LABOR

BATTLEGROUND

LABOR BATTLEGROUND

The Streets of Chicago

Doug Nelson

Chicago History Series
Chicago, Illinois 60601

Copyright 1996 by Doug Nelson

All rights reserved.
Printed in the United States of America
First Printing

Chicago History Series
200 N. LaSalle Suite 100
Chicago, Illinois 60601

```
             Library of Congress Cataloging-in-Publication Data


Nelson, Doug, 1950 July 24
    Labor battleground : the streets of Chicago / Doug Nelson.
       p.   cm.
    Includes bibliographical references and index.
    ISBN 1-878386-03-4
    1. Labor movement--Illinois--Chicago--History.  2. Strikes and
lockouts--Illinois--Chicago--History.  3. Working class--Illinois-
-Chicago--History.  4. Trade-unions--Illinois--Chicago--History.
  I. Title.
HD8085.C53N45   1995
331.89'2977311--dc20                                      95-12972
                                                              CIP
```

Cover Picture
The Memorial Day Massacre at Republic Steel.

In May, 1937, striking steelworkers marched against a police contingent guarding the mill located on the southeast side of Chicago. A total of 10 strikers were killed in the confrontation.

Illustration by John Downs

This book is dedicated to John Peter Altgeld, Governor of Illinois from 1893 - 1897, who took many unpopular stands regardless of the political consequences. In 1893 Governor Altgeld pardoned the anarchists imprisoned as a result of the Haymarket Square riot even though he knew it would end his political career. He also opposed President Cleveland's sending of federal troops to Pullman in 1894 to break that strike.

ACKNOWLEDGEMENTS

There were many individuals and organizations which helped with gathering the material in this book. Several trade unions helped. I would like to thank the Chicago Lodge of the Fraternal Order of Police, specifically Harold Kunz and Bob Podgorny, for their help on this project. I am indebted to Ellen Schur Brown of the Chicago Teachers Union for her contributions. I thank Steve Berman of the Typographical Union for his material on the Tribune strike. I also wish to thank Larry Matkaitis of the Chicago Fire Department, who was a official with the Chicago Fire Fighters Union during the strike, for providing valuable information. However, any conclusions and judgements on this material are entirely my own.

I wish to thank Pete O'Day, my co-author of *WORKPLACE 2000*, for reviewing the draft of this book and providing valuable comments. John Downs did an excellent job providing illustrations for the cover and many of the chapters in the book. The staffs of the Chicago Public Library, Chicago Historical Society, and the Illinois State Historical Library all provided valuable assistance. Photographs with the designation of (CHS) have been supplied by the Chicago Historical Society.

ABOUT THE AUTHOR

Doug Nelson is on the staff of the Illinois Department of Labor. Before joining the Department of Labor he worked in the steel industry on the south side of Chicago for fourteen years. He was an elected steelworker union representative for ten years. His educational background includes a History degree from Portland State University in Portland, Oregon and a graduate degree from the University of Illinois in Chicago. He is on the faculty of the University of Illinois and also teaches at South Suburban College in South Holland, Illinois.

LABOR BATTLEGROUND is Doug Nelson's second book. He was a co-author with Pete O'Day of *WORKPLACE 2000* which is about worker self management teams in industrial environments.

TABLE OF CONTENTS

		PAGE
INTRODUCTION		10
CHAPTER 1	CONFLICT BEGINS	11
	BEER AND BLOOD (1855)	12
	EIGHT HOURS FOR WHAT WE WILL (1867)	15
	BREAD OR BLOOD (1873)	20
CHAPTER 2	ATTEMPTS TO ORGANIZE ARE MET WITH VIOLENCE	25
	BATTLE OF THE VIADUCT (1877)	26
	STREETCAR STRIKE (1885)	31
	HAYMARKET SQUARE (1886)	33
CHAPTER 3	REFORM AND EARLY TRADE UNION BATTLES	47
	PULLMAN STRIKE (1894)	48
	TEAMSTER STRIKE (1902)	59
	TEAMSTER STRIKE (1905)	60
	STREETCAR STRIKES (1903)	67
	MEATPACKER STRIKE (1904)	70
	GARMENT WORKERS STRIKE (1910)	74
	GARMENT WORKERS STRIKE (1915)	76
	HENRICI STRIKES (1914)	78
CHAPTER 4	BATTLE TO ORGANIZE INDUSTRY	82
	RACE AND LABOR WAR IN CHICAGO (1919)	83
	MEATPACKING STRIKE (1921)	89
	MOB INFLUENCE IN THE UNIONS (1930s)	92
	MEMORIAL DAY MASSACRE (1937)	95
CHAPTER 5	POST WAR RETREAT	110
	RADICAL STRIKE AGAINST HARVESTER (1952)	111
	STEEL INDUSTRY AND UNION IN TRANSITION (1970s)	116
	CHICAGO TRIBUNE STRIKE (1985)	118
CHAPTER 6	ORGANIZATION IN THE PUBLIC SECTOR	123
	CHICAGO TEACHERS UNION (1967)	124
	BROTHERS OF THE BARREL (1980)	128
	FIRST CHICAGO POLICE CONTRACT (1981)	133
LIST OF ABBREVIATIONS USED		136
APPENDIX A	TIMELINE	137

TABLE OF CONTENTS (cont.) PAGE

APPENDIX B   HISTORICAL DOCUMENTS

    B-1 THE EIGHT HOUR DAY LAW (1867)............ 139
    B-2 GUN CONTROL LAW (1879).................. 140
    B-3 *CROSS OF GOLD* SPEECH (1896)............ 141
    B-4 *WHY TEACHERS SHOULD ORGANIZE* (1904).... 145
    B-5 REPUBLIC STEEL LETTER TO WORKERS (1936)... 150
         FIRST STEELWORKER LABOR AGREEMENT (1937).. 152
    B-6 LABOR RELATIONS ACT FOR THE PUBLIC
         SECTOR (1984)........................... 155

APPENDIX C   SELECTED SOURCES AND FURTHER READING........... 157

INDEX   159

LIST OF DRAWINGS, MAPS, AND PICTURES PAGE

1-1 Crowds surround the Courthouse for Lager Beer trial...... 14
1-2 Eight-hour movement supporters attempt to stop work...... 17
1-3 Crowds surround the Relief and Aid Society.............. 23

2-1 Troops and crowds fight in the railroad years........... 28
2-2 Crowds attack and destroy a street car.................. 32
2-3 Police attack strikers at McCormick Works............... 35
2-4 Haymarket *Revenge* flyer............................... 37
2-5 Haymarket *Attention Workingmen!* flyer................. 38
2-6 Map of Haymarket Square................................. 40
2-7 Haymarket explosion..................................... 42
2-8 Scene of Haymarket explosion............................ 43
2-9 Haymarket Monument...................................... 45

3-1 Jane Addams' Hull-House................................. 49
3-2 Map of area where Troops and Pullman strikers fought.... 53
3-3 Troops fire into strikers at 49th/Loomis................ 54
3-4 Police clash with crowd at 113th St..................... 55
3-5 Crowd setting fire to train cars........................ 56
3-6 Police fire at strikers................................. 57
3-7 Wrecked freight cars at 104th St........................ 58
3-8 Teamsters overturn delivery wagons (CHS)................ 61
3-9 Newspaper cartoon of use of blacks in the strike........ 63
3-10 Police break strike blockade............................ 63
3-11 Montgomery Ward advertisement about strike.............. 64
3-12 Police escorting wagons................................. 65
3-13 Fulton and Jefferson blockade........................... 65
3-14 IWW organization.. 66
3-15 Newspaper cartoon of Streetcar strike of 1903........... 68
3-16 Meatcutter union flyer to members....................... 71
3-17 Strikers attack meat wagon.............................. 73
3-18 Union members picket clothing maker (CHS)............... 75

LIST OF DRAWINGS, MAPS, AND PICTURES (cont.)

		PAGE
3-19	Waitress' Union pickets Henrici Restaurant	79
3-20	Handbill which union handed out to promote boycott	80
4-1	Map of fire and riot zone	84
4-2	Burned out neighborhood and its residents	85
4-3	Flyer by Steel union stating demands	87
4-4	Flyer by Steel union calling for meeting during strike	88
4-5	Police attack strikers at the Swift meatpacking plant	90
4-6	Jack Ruby arrested in connection with union killing	93
4-7	Flyer by Steel union attacking company unions	96
4-8	First picket line at Republic Steel	96
4-9	Strike headquarters - Sam's Place (CHS)	98
4-10	Strike rally on Memorial Day (CHS)	99
4-11	Strikers march to plant on Memorial Day (CHS)	100
4-12	Map of Republic Steel area	101
4-13	Police await marchers as they approach plant	103
4-14	Picture taken at moment bloodshed begins	103
4-15	Police club marchers	104
4-16	Police follow marchers as they retreat	104
4-17	Police club wounded marchers	105
4-18	Police do not allow medical attention to wounded	106
4-19	Hilding Anderson dying	107
4-20	Strikers at mass protest rally	107
4-21	Speakers at mass protest rally	107
4-22	Union notice of funeral services	109
5-1	Union advertisement listing reasons for strike	112
5-2	Company advertisement attacking union leaders	113
5-3	Rally against strikebreakers outside plant	114
5-4	Car driven by worker which was set afire by union	114
5-5	Newsletter about USWA District Director election	117
5-6	Flyer by Printers' Union asking for *Tribune* boycott	120
5-7	Photo of Tribune truck covered by union signs	121
5-8	Coupon used by union to cancel subscriptions	121
6-1	Teachers demonstrate at City Hall in 1934 (CHS)	126
6-2	Union mascot joining picket line	130
6-3	Sign at Fire Fighters rally	130
6-4	Police at commemoration Haymarket Square Monument	134

INTRODUCTION

The purpose of this book is to provide a popular history of significant labor events in Chicago history. While the city of Chicago has been strongly unionized, this book is meant to be a history of events in Chicago involving working people whether unions were directly involved or not. Most books which have been written focus on one event or another (Haymarket and the Pullman strike being the most popular). These books do not attempt to give an overall history. As a result many important events are unknown, even to Chicago area residents.

Illinois state law requires schools to teach labor history and the roles unions have played. This book is an attempt to help in that effort. Many books which have been written are academic in nature and do not relate to the popular reader. This book is written in the style that can be read by High School students and those with a high school education. Many pictures, maps and drawings are included.

The main section of the book is divided into six chapters. The first chapter covers the period just before and after the Civil War in Chicago, when a mainly foreign born population came into conflict with City Hall's attempts to bring order and create a business climate. The second chapter reviews violent battles against government and business which were largely led by unorganized groups or anarchists. The third chapter reports on the early attempts by trade unions to gain recognition in industry at the turn of the century. Chapter four covers the period after World War I and before World War II. This period saw some of the worst bloodshed in Chicago as unions fought for inroads in basic industry. As unions became successful organized crime corrupted some of the unions. The fifth chapter reviews significant labor battles after World War II in the private sector. This has been a period of little growth and even retreat in some industries. The final chapter covers the post-World War II labor organizing which has taken place in the public sector. In the last forty years the only large gains labor has made has been among public sector occupations. There has been very little written about these efforts to organize and gain contract recognition among the teachers, fire fighters and police.

The final section of the book gives a timeline of events, a reference bibliography, and reprints of historical documents. The documents that have been reprinted come from the different historical periods and originated in response to Chicago events in these historical periods.

CONFLICT

BEGINS

1

BEER AND BLOOD (1855)

Chicago's first bloody battle between the police and angry crowds took place at the end of a decade when Chicago turned from a frontier town into a modern city. In the early 1840s Chicago was a rapidly expanding town on the Northwest frontier. The city's first detailed census in 1844 showed a population of 7600. Just three years later the city had almost 15,000 residents. Most of the growth was immigrants from Ireland and Germany. As this growth continued, anti-foreign feelings increased, particularly among the developing business community. There was a fear that immigrants would destroy American values. This fear also took on an anti-Catholic tone because of the religious background of most of the new arrivals. Nationally this attitude manifested itself in the formation of the Native American Party. This party became known as the Know-Nothings because the members said 'they knew nothing' in response to questions about their activities.

Early in the year 1847 Chicago congressman Wentworth organized a meeting which brought almost 3,000 delegates to the city. The intent of the meeting was to have business people from other states see the area and learn how they could make money. In this period Chicago was an open town with very few police. It was a center of gambling in the West and most crime went unreported. This was about to change. The city's political structure wanted to be able to exercise control over the foreign born population and make the town safe for the development of business. By February 1855, the police force had tripled to three units, each consisting of 35 men.

Both nationally and in Chicago there were movements for temperance particularly as it applied to the foreign born. In 1851 the Illinois legislature passed a law forbidding the sale of liquor in containers less than a one quart. This law did not allow a tavern to sell liquor that would be drank at the tavern. Newspapers such as the *Chicago Tribune* blamed trouble in the city on drinking by Irish Catholics.

In March 1854, a candidate of the Know Nothings was defeated for Mayor. The Know Nothings blamed their defeat on Catholic priests, Irish and German drinkers, and the taverns. The next year the Know Nothings elected Levi D. Boone, a relative of the famed explorer Daniel Boone, as Mayor. He immediately raised the saloon fees from $50 to $300 a year. He also started enforcement of an old law which would close the taverns on Sundays. This particularly enraged the Germans. By this time almost 25,000 Germans had fled their country, after failure of the 1848 revolution, and came to Chicago. Sunday was usually their only day off and they would go to the tavern to eat, for recreation, talk politics and drink. In 1855 Germans and Irish owned over 92% of the city's taverns.

German tavern owners refused to (or could not) pay the increased license fees. The newly increased police force began to make dozens of arrests when taverns operated on Sundays. Tavern owners began to organize opposition and hold meetings. Chicago's local press played up these meetings and tried to alarm the local population. Mayor Boone sent the police, armed with guns (not common at the time), to arrest many of the owners. Eventually about 200 owners and employees were arrested. Those who tried to resist were beaten.

The large number of arrests led to a logjam at the Cook County Court House. Both sides in the dispute decided to consolidate the cases and set the trial for April 21, 1855. Newspapers printed rumors of civic uprising as the date neared. The morning of April 21 about 400 Germans marched south from the North side across the Clark Street bridge. They assembled in front of the lager saloons across Randolph Street from the Court House. Many in the crowd followed the defendants into the courthouse. The courtroom was packed and the people filled the halls outside. At 11 AM the judge ordered the crowd out. Officers attempted to clear the courthouse and pushed the mob down into the streets. At this point the intersection of Randolph and Clark was filled halting traffic.

A platoon of police led by the Captain of Police, Luther Nichols, attacked the crowd with clubs. As some officers fired pistols the demonstrators started to fall back up Clark Street. By noon the police captured eight marchers and drove the crowd back across the Clark Street bridge. The Mayor ordered the bridge to be swung open in order to prevent the crowd from returning.

Soon rumors came from the North side that there was 5000 Germans who were armed and ready to march. Informants said the group planned to free those arrested and burn City Hall. The Mayor ordered all police to be brought in and the sheriff moved to deputize 200 men whom he got from nearby stores and warehouses. At 3 PM at least 1000 Germans marched through the near North side. Their weapons included shotguns, pistols, clubs and other items.

NEXT PAGE

An angry crowd gathers at the Cook County Courthouse as the trial begins.

At 4 PM the Clark Street drawbridge had to be shut to let traffic across the river. At this time 150 men ran across the bridge and down Clark. Waving their weapons, they broke up into two groups which charged into three platoons of police and the men who had been newly deputized.

Some in the crowd shouted "to shoot out the stars" and gunfire erupted on both sides. A German fired his shotgun resulting in an officer losing his arm. The assailant, Peter Martin, was immediately shot as he ran and he was killed. The battle continued for almost one hour and finally the Germans, along with some Irish, withdrew across the bridge to the North side. There were 19 serious injuries at the scene and some of these died within the next few days. The number of fatalities is unknown as the men were buried secretly.

Militia units from the volunteer Light Guard arrived to surround the courthouse area. A total of 60 marchers were arrested during the fighting and afterward. The city was in a state of shock at this turn of events. Eventually a total of 14 went on trial but no one ever was sent to jail. The city stopped enforcing the Sunday closing ordinance. The final casualty of the "Beer Riots" was the state prohibition law which went down to defeat two weeks later with the margin against especially heavy in Chicago.

EIGHT HOURS FOR WHAT WE WILL (1867)

A generation before the Haymarket bomb disrupted the eight-hour movement of the 1880s, workers battled over the issue in Chicago. Attempts to shorten the workday were made frequently in the nineteenth century. Quality of life for the average working person could only be increased by the reduction of hours of work. Often the struggle to limit working hours went back and forth according to the economic health of developing American business. In the early part of the 19th century skilled workers saw their working hours drop to ten per day. This benefit was lost by 1840 because of recession. In the following 20 years, as the industrial working population increased, most states passed laws limiting the workday to ten hours. These laws didn't apply to large factories but there were very few of those in mid-nineteenth century America.

In Chicago, after the Civil War, the local economy was somewhat distorted. Many people had made money from the sale of war materiel. As a result prices continued to rise as they had during the war. However when the war ended orders fell and many people saw their wages drop. Many jobs disappeared completely. By 1867 there were 175,000 foreign born workers in Chicago.

Workers soon began calling for the eight-hour day. Illinois became one of the first states to pass an eight-hour day law. This law, **reprinted in Appendix B-1**, contained a loophole. The law didn't apply to employment contracts, which could set any hours of work. This law did not set a means of enforcement, which meant it would only be enforced with pressure from the workers.

As the first of May neared, when the law was to take effect, labor organizations began to hold meetings to decide how to enforce the act. Manufacturing companies began to complain they would be driven out of business if they gave in to the demands. They said companies in the countryside could sell their products at 20% cheaper. Machine shop owners said the eastern factories could sell at a lower cost.

Newspapers began to report that men were being fired when they said they stood for the eight-hour day. Other shops followed the example of the Eagle Works. This machine shop gave its men a flyer that said:

> **After fully weighing this subject in their own minds, if a sufficient number of our men to warrant running are willing to work ten hours a day, as heretofore, being paid by the hour, and will so indicate in writing or otherwise, we shall go as usual; but if determined otherwise, we shall only continue a force sufficient to close up the business with the least possible loss; and each person will, before commencing after May 1st, be expected to indicate his acceptance of this proposition.**
>
> *Tribune* April 30, 1867

Some labor organizations attempted to work a compromise with their employers. It was felt that unless some movement was made toward the bosses the eight-hour movement might prove to be a failure. The Journeymen Painters passed a resolution that stated:

> *Resolved*. **That we, the journeymen painters of Chicago, are willing to meet our employers half way -- eight hours work for nine hours pay.**

This resolution was immediately voted down by the employer organization. They passed another that said that pay would be cut by 20% if the men wanted to work eight hours.

When May 1 came, a Wednesday, thousands walked off their jobs. The trade unions scheduled a march through the principal streets of each division of the city. This route was seven and one half miles long and would end on the lakefront, where Randolph

OPPOSITE PAGE

Battles erupted in Bridgeport lumber yards as the supporters of the Eight-Hour movement attempted to stop work.

and Lake Shore Drive are today. Those unions participating were a cross section of workers in 1867 Chicago. They included the:

> **Stonecutters' Union**
> **Moulders' Union**
> **Plumbers' Union**
> **Plasters' Union**
> **Ship Carpenters' and Caulkers' Union**
> **Chicago Seamens' Union**
> **Steam and Gas Fitters' Union**
> **Brass Finishers' Union**
> **Cigar Makers' Union**
> **Laborers' Benevolent Association**
> **Carpenters' and Joiners' Union**
> **MarbleCutters' Union**
> **Shoemakers' Union**
> **Painters' Union**
> **Tanners' and Curriers' Union**
> **Upholsterers' Union**
> **Mill Finishers' Union**
> **Coachmakers' Union**
> **German Bricklayers**
> **Lock Manufacturers**
> **Illinois Central Shops and Car Works**
> **Northwestern Railway Shops**

There were an estimated 10,000 participants for the parade. The march wound through the streets with each union, group or organization carrying their banners and pictures. It was windy and liberal clouds of dust covered the marchers. The Tanners Union carried a banner decorated with ribbons and picturing President Grant. Four horses drew the Moulders' Union truck. It was covered by a white banner which read:

> *Let it roll along our prairie,*
> *Let it roll o'er dare and hill;*
> *Eight hours for work, eight hours for rest,*
> *Eight hours for what we will.*

When the march ended at the lake there were three stands set up for the audience. Two stands were for English speakers and one stand was for German speakers. Mayor Rice presided at the meeting and drew cheers when he said:

The Streets of Chicago

It is said in some books that the interests of labor and capital are mutual. I do not believe it. I believe they are antagonistic. The workingman desires the highest price for his labor. The capitalist wants that labor performed at the lowest possible sum.

Most could not hear any of the speakers but the main purpose of the gathering was to organize the continuing general strike. The day was one of festivity unlike the days to follow.

At 9 AM, the next day, about 400 men gathered at Polk and the Lakefront. Several committees were appointed to go to the different shops and factories to find out whether the men were working eight or ten hours. If they were working ten hours the committees were to convince men still working to walk out. If they resisted force was used. Most places these committees visited resulted in the suspension of work. At 11 AM the committees joined and started visiting factories as a "committee of the whole." This crowd swept through the lumber mills on the southwest side of the city (the area south of Eighteenth Street and south and west of the Chicago River). Work was shut down and the mob gathered sticks and other materials from the yards to use elsewhere.

As the afternoon approached the Bridgeport district was completely in the hands of the committees. Work had come to a halt with several workers beaten and severely injured when they tried to resist the crowd. The police detachment, which only numbered 20 men, was outnumbered and withdrew without fighting.

Friday, May 3, most of the lumber mills and other construction shops had been shut down. The violence diminished as the police increased their presence. As with the day before there were very few arrests. The police were unwilling to go into the crowds to pick individuals out. About 200 men went along Archer Avenue visiting places they had covered the day before. Any that were still open they shut down.

Chicago's largest factory, the McCormick Reaper works, was largely unaffected. The factory was well protected and men there continued to work a ten-hour day. Management did offer a 10 percent wage increase after May 1.

The beginning of the next work week saw many workers return to their jobs. Most of the crowds that had shut down work lacked any direction or leadership and thus were destined to fail. Work finally resumed on May 13. The eight-hour movement shifted to the courts and trade union meetings. As the next decade dawned, recession came and the eight-hour day disappeared at most places where it had been won. It would be almost 20 years later before the issue would again come to the streets.

LABOR BATTLEGROUND

BREAD OR BLOOD (1873)

Chicago's great fire in October 1871, destroyed the entire business district and most of the North side residential area. Over 100,000 were left homeless and the property loss was $200 million. Only $90 million was covered by insurance and only half was paid. Almost 100 insurance companies of the 250 doing business in Chicago failed rather than pay.

The story of this destruction quickly went around the world. Contributions came not only from the rest of the states but from Europe as well. Over five million dollars came in with one million from foreign countries. At today's rates this was equivalent to two billion dollars. Mayor Mason decided to form a private group known as the Relief and Aid Society that was directed by Chicago businessmen. The Relief Society would decide how the money would be spent.

Within a month of the fire almost 50,000 persons were receiving relief at distribution points. There were 15,000 loaves of bread provided free by Chicago bakeries on a daily basis. This season of good feeling only lasted a short time. Two weeks after the fire the *Tribune* complained about men who were hanging around churches waiting for relief supplies. An editorial urged a "no-work, no-eat policy." The amount of money flowing from the relief societies began to ebb.

Chicago immediately began to rebuild and 10,000 structures were built by the end of 1872. Workers from Europe came to participate in the building explosion. This activity brought along its own problems with the death rate in 1872 higher than the year before. This was due to the poor sanitary conditions of the working-class areas.

After the initial construction boom leveled off Chicago was in a recession. Insects caused a disastrous loss for grain crops in the Midwest. On top of that the nation's largest investment house, Jay Cooke and Company, failed in September 1873 creating a currency panic. The Panic of 1873 caused business losses in the U.S. of 200 million dollars; an amount that was equal to the losses suffered during the Chicago fire. These poor economic conditions, combined with the harsh winter of 1873, caused many people to die of hunger and the cold.

Many began to complain the Relief and Aid Society was sitting on its money, nearly $600,000, and should increase distribution. Sunday night, December 21, 1873, there was a meeting at Turner's Hall on Twelfth and Halsted with 6,000 present. Leaders spoke in German, Polish and English denouncing the lack of aid or work available. The speakers urged the crowd to demand work from the city. They also requested those assembled to show up at the city council Monday night to pressure the aldermen. Those at the meeting decided to march and appoint a committee to present their demands to the council the next evening.

The Streets of Chicago

The next night the crowd at Washington and Union grew to 10,000. At the front of the march were two flags, an American and a Red banner. Many marchers carried banners with slogans reading:

One for All and All for One.
United We Stand, Divided We Fall.
Einigkeit Macht Stark (Unity Gives Strength).
Krieg dem Muesaiggang (War to Idleness).
Work or Bread.
Tod der Noth (Death to Destitution).

A detachment of police marched ahead of the crowd. The leadership of the crowd ordered the march halted at the intersection of Des Plaines and Adams but the police didn't realize the march had stopped and kept going until they got to City Hall. The marchers then split into four groups to avoid being stopped by the police. One group went over the Madison street bridge, one went over at Randolph, the third through the Washington street tunnel and the final division went over Adams street bridge.

The four groups surrounded the Relief and Aid Society headquarters at the northeast corner of Randolph and LaSalle. City Hall was barricaded by police but the workingmen's organizations were allowed to fill the council chambers. Mr. F.A.Hoffman, who was chairman of the workingmen's committees who met Sunday at Turner Hall, spoke to the council. He demanded work on city projects, relief when no work was available, disbursements made by a worker's committee and when the city did not have cash it should issue credit. One alderman immediately promised all the bread needed for the next six months, and the city could pay him when it could.

The mayor demanded the director of the Relief Society give an accounting of relief extended in the last two weeks. The report stated there were assets of $580,000. In the first half of December the Society distributed the following:

Money

539 cash appropriations	$ 5,476
353 tons of soft coal	1,939
9 tons of hard coal	90
3 cords of wood	30

Articles

Mens wear	70
Children's wear	182
Pairs of shoes	281
Pairs of blankets	109

Meals

Tickets for board and lodging	20
For single meals	236
For single lodging	91
Lodging at free lodging-house	450

Employment

Those furnished with employment	152
The total aided by cash or coal	904

A resolution was passed by the Council that called on the Relief Society to distribute more funds. This effort would be helped by the Mayor and three aldermen.

Over the next few days negotiations continued between the Relief Society, the Workingmen's organization and City Hall. Unlike the tone of Monday's demonstration, which was peaceful, the leaders began to threaten each other. Papers in the city compared the situation to the Paris Bread riot of 1848 (*Chicago Times*) and used headlines like "Our Communists" (*Chicago Tribune*).

Marches continued to the Relief Society. The Society would not agree to turn over funding to the city council. At the beginning of the next week the Society agreed to increase its distribution of relief. Mail applications were allowed so that crowding would decrease.

The workingmens' organizations felt they should organize a permanent political party so they would be represented in the future. Participants were mainly Germans and Scandinavians. A platform was adopted calling for:

1) **Transportation and communications operated by the state;**
2) **Banks and insurance operated by the state;**
3) **End monopoly legislation;**
4) **Pass stronger laws for the recovery of unpaid wages;**
5) **Stop the leasing of prison labor for industrial or construction work; and**
6) **Compulsory education from 7 to 14, with no child labor under 14.**

This party, the Workingmens's Party of Illinois was created January 11, 1874.

OPPOSITE PAGE

Crowds surround the Relief and Aid Society at Randolph and LaSalle

Demonstrations and marches continued over the next couple years until the money gave out in **1876**. This initial "Bread Riot" in December **1873** helped create political organizations that would lead laborers in Chicago for the next two decades. Marching and drill units were formed and speeches of hatred between the classes were commonly heard. These forces would result in ever increasing violence in Chicago as the century closed.

ATTEMPTS

TO ORGANIZE

ARE MET WITH

VIOLENCE

2

THE BATTLE OF THE VIADUCT (1877)

The Panic of 1873 sparked a decade of economic hard times. Prominent people, such as the President of Chicago's Union National Bank, William Coolbaugh, blew their brains out. Average working people showed their resentment by striking. The Great Railway Strike of 1877 connected small and large cities across the nation in a united effort unlike any seen in the country's history to that point. In the Chicago area the lasting monument to this battle would be the construction of Fort Sheridan and the Great Lakes Naval base (more on this later in the chapter). Never again would there be a city-wide upheaval of this magnitude.

The expansion of the West was fueled by the expansion of the nation's railroads. Many large corporations were formed as railroad companies joined together. Monopolies were created as the railroads divided up areas of the country. In a particular area one company could dominate and set the rates or divide up traffic. Railroads also helped create a national marketplace and provided the demand for raw materials for developing industries of iron and coal.

In early 1877 the major railroads joined in an agreement to restrict wages in the industry. Railroad workers had already been through a number of wages cuts in the 1870s. Strikes to protest these actions had been defeated in 1873 and 1874. When the Baltimore and Ohio instituted a 15 percent wage cut on July 16, workers in Martinsburg, West Virginia walked off the job. Strikers easily outnumbered the limited police in the area and no one could be found to break the strike. This success started to spread from railway yard to railway yard, and from town to city. Business leaders felt there was an insurrection in the making. Violence erupted in Baltimore, Buffalo, and Pittsburgh. President Hayes called out federal troops to meet the strikers in West Virginia.

The Streets of Chicago

Federal troops had initial success in breaking the strike in Martinsburg but area locals started to attack the trains. Led by coal miners crowds attacked a train coming out of Martinsburg. Even though the train was guarded by 75 federal troops it was halted.

In Chicago the railroad workers had received a 16 percent pay cut on July 1. The pay of engineers was reduced from 65 dollars to 55 dollars per month. The helper's pay went from 50 to 42 dollars per month. News of the railroad violence in Baltimore and West Virginia began reaching Chicago on July 18. By July 21 the news of the military taking action in Pittsburgh moved the new of the Russian-Turkish war off the front pages. The next day meetings were held in city neighborhoods. At 20th and Brown streets, Sack's Hall, the Workingmen's Party held a meeting at which Albert Parsons spoke. He gave a speech attacking capitalism and urged those present to organize. The group issued the following proclamation:

> **To all Sections of the Workingmen's Party of the United States:**
>
> **COMRADES: In the desperate struggle for existence now being maintained by the workingmen of the great railroads throughout the land, we expect that every member will render all possible moral and substantial assistance to our brethren, and support all reasonable measures which may be found necessary by them.**
>
> **The Executive Committee**
> **Philip Van Patten, Corresponding Secretary**
> **Chicago, July 22d, 1877**

During this time the city was preparing to deal with mob action. The New York Herald reported that Chicago's Mayor Heath did not fear the "Irish or Germans" but was concerned about the "Bohemians who inhabit the lumber district". Rifles were sent to police station houses and one unit received cannons.

On July 23 a meeting was held in Market Square, between Madison and Washington streets near Halsted, at which Albert Parsons again spoke. They called themselves the "Grand Army of Starvation" and nine thousand were present. Parsons said they would return the fire of military. He wanted the military disbanded and he attacked labor-saving machinery. Most of the crowd was laborers, lumber-yard workers and teenagers. There were few railroad workers taking part.

NEXT PAGE

Troops and strikers fight in South side railroad yards.

The Streets of Chicago

Finally the railroad men in Chicago struck on Monday night July 23. The Michigan Central was closed first and then a group closed the Illinois Central yards. Now the "delegation" numbered 400 and they went to other depots to enforce a strike. In quick order the Baltimore & Ohio, Burlington, and Rock Island were all shut down.

Now the crowds broke up into different groups. They went to the lumber yards, mills, and factories attempting to close them down. Many of the workers were forced to become part of the crowds. At the lumber yards the crowds collected weapons consisting of clubs and sticks. One group marched down 22nd street shutting down the wood working mills in that area.

The crowds moved back and forth in the area bounded from the lake to the edge of the city at Western Avenue. Gun stores were a favorite target. The mayor ordered gun shops and pawnbrokers to remove their weapons and ammunition. The mayor further requested:

> **...the citizens organize patrols in their respective neighborhoods, and keep their women and children off the public highways...The city government has made ample preparation to protect the lives and property of all citizens, and any lawless acts will be promptly detected and punished.**
>
> **M. Heath, Mayor, July 24th, 1877**

Liquor stores and taverns were also ordered closed by the mayor at the same time. City leaders went on the offensive and organized a meeting the next day, Wednesday afternoon July 25, at the Moody Tabernacle. Over 50,000 packed the meeting at which Mayor Heath requested, "the raising of a force of five thousand good and experienced citizens composed mainly of ex-soldiers to put down the ragged Commune wrenches".

At the same time as the Tabernacle meeting a crowd joined railroad strikers at the Burlington shops on Sixteenth street. Stones were thrown at the buildings and a attempt was made to burn them. Several engines and cars were pushed off the tracks by the mob which had grown to three thousand. A police unit approached the crowd and they were met with a barrage of stones. Police returned fire with revolvers and in 45 minutes seven of the crowd were killed and 36 seriously wounded. Fourteen of the police were seriously injured. At this point the police ran out of ammunition and retreated north on Halsted. Encouraged, the mob went up and down Halsted destroying street cars and looting a gun shop. They retrieved 200 revolvers and shotguns along with several barrels of powder.

During Wednesday twelve companies of U.S. Army 9th Infantry troops came to Chicago. These troops were fresh from the Indian wars in the West. The next morning, July 26, Illinois Governor Cullom asked the President for U.S. troops. The

President ordered troops under General Sheridan's command to be used by the Governor and Mayor to put down the riot.

Thursday morning a meeting was called by carpenters and cabinet makers to discuss the eight hour day among other issues. About 200 were present at Turner Hall on Twelfth street which was a block from the police station. Two squads of police decided to break up the meeting. There was no apparent reason for this other than general mob action in the area. Twenty five police approached the Hall and people started throwing bricks and stones as the officers stood on the street. They began to attack the crowd moving into the Hall. At this point another 20 police joined the battle. The workers inside panicked and tried to flee. Furniture was thrown out of windows to create escape routes. One worker was killed, many were wounded with two police injured. Later the workers sued the police and achieved a partial victory because of a lack of provocation.

While the fighting was taking place at Turner Hall another battle was shaping up along Halsted street. A crowd had formed at the Halsted street viaduct which passed over the railroad tracks at Sixteenth street. Railroad cars were being stoned and fired upon. A police commander, Joseph Dixon, had put a cannon on a wagon and with this artillery forced the crowd off the viaduct. The crowd returned in a couple hours and now numbered 10,000. They began to shower police with stones and other missiles from roofs and alleyways. Police fired on the crowd but soon ran out of ammunition and retreated. The viaduct was retaken by the crowd. At this point the crowd split into two directions going east and west along Sixteenth street.

The police formed a new line and charged again. The size of the crowd got the better of the police and soon they had to retreat. The police fled north across the viaduct. As they reached Fifteenth street they were almost overrun but a regiment of cavalry appeared and attacked the mob. As the crowd fled the combination of police and troops of the Second Illinois Regiment fired hitting many. The final toll of the 'Battle of the Viaduct' was 16 dead from the crowd and nine police were wounded. Many more dead were carried off by others.

The arrival of federal troops cooled the week of disorganized strike related violence. After these defeats radical and socialist elements of Chicago's working class saw the limits of spontaneity. The socialists began to organize military companies and marched openly with weapons. Anarchists, going the other direction, began to practice bomb-making. Individuals and groups would travel to areas outside of Chicago, such as the Indiana dunes, to set bombs off and measure the effects.

On March 22, 1879 the socialist military groups held a great demonstration in the Exposition Hall. Almost 40,000 attended the military brigade fundraiser. Soon after a law was passed by the Illinois legislature banning public marching by these groups.

The law, which established the Illinois National Guard, also banned people from organizing themselves into military-type groups.

This repressive law, which was meant as a form of gun control for workers, is reprinted as **Appendix B-2**.

STREET CAR STRIKE (1885)

The street car strike began June 30, 1885. This strike involved some of the same people and forces that would clash the next year at Haymarket. The city saw violence in the business and financial district which had not occurred in Chicago. Crowds threw stones at cars in operation on the streets. Three or four people would jump on the cars and uncouple the cars from the horses. There were incidents where up to 3000 people would attack and destroy cars.

There were three demands of the strikers: 1) Increase and Equalize Pay; 2) Dismiss an abusive assistant superintendent; and 3) Decrease the time of Probation. A meeting was held in early June to press the above demands. The company complied with the demands, firing the supervisor, increasing pay and reducing probation from 60 to 30 days. The very next day 15 men were fired including three of the Committee of ten which had presented the demands. These employees were officers of the Conductors Benevolent & Protective Association.

In this strike the non-economic issue of the integrity of the union became primary. Mayor Harrison suggested arbitration but the companies rejected this request. The car barns were located on Western and Madison streets. The police found it physically impossible to monitor the 400 cars on 45 miles of roads. Main lines ran along Lake, Randolph, Madison, and State streets. Some of the most violent conflict took place in the Madison and Halsted area. The companies hired scabs and the crowds pulled them off the cars and beat them. On Friday, July 3, the police tried to run the street cars. Police arrested 121 strikers and were accused of beating many of them. Captain Bonfield was the main police commander who was accused of brutality by the strikers. He would surface the next year as one of the commanders at Haymarket Square.

In order to stop the streetcars strikers would rip up sewer traps along the streets to disrupt the traffic. Neighborhoods and street crowds were very supportive of the strikers. The Mayor said that the majority of the city population was in favor of the strikers. The city riders had complaints of unclean cars with poor ventilation. Crowds would hide strikers from the police after acts of violence were committed.

NEXT PAGE

Crowds destroy streetcars along Randolph Street.

The Streets of Chicago

Many of the city leaders began to worry this strike would lead to a repeat of the death and violence of 1877. On the July 4 holiday too many police were needed for July 4 picnics and were unable to run the cars. That day, Saturday, the Mayor wrote and again asked for arbitration. He said each side should pick a Cook County judge and those tow would pick a third. Sunday July 5 the strikers held a rally. August Spies spoke and said, "The day is coming when the people will have to face bayonets and they must be prepared". He said if the cars ran on Monday they should arm themselves with bricks.

On Monday, the Chicago city council met and passed a resolution against the companies and formed a committee to investigate the strike. The strike was settled on Tuesday July 7. The company President, Mr. Jones, agreed to fire the strikebreakers and review the cases of the 16 discharged men. This strike caused business leaders to increase the police force and begin forming associations which would solidify the financial community.

HAYMARKET SQUARE (1886)

In 1884 the Federation of Organized Trades and Labor Unions, which evolved into the American Federation of Labor, called for an eight-hour day starting May 1, 1886. In Chicago the Illinois State Federation of Labor met on March 26 of that year. This group passed a resolution that demanded an "enactment and enforcement of a law making eight hours a legal days work". This resolution also fixed May 1, 1886 as a goal. A shorter work day was a goal of labor organizations for many decades previously. Eight hour legislation had been passed in several states (see Chapter 1 and Appendix B-1). These laws contained loopholes and were never seriously enforced.

In the Spring of 1886 there were demonstrations around the country for the eight-hour day. The Knights of Labor was the largest workers group in the nation and it's leadership opposed the eight hour movement as a distraction. Local chapters of the Knights of Labor generally ignored their national leaders and promoted a general strike to enforce the eight hour day. This would be the first national general strike in United States history. Among the local leaders of the Knights of Labor in Chicago was former Confederate army veteran Albert Parsons. Parsons and his wife Lucy had arrived in Chicago in 1873 and became leaders among the radicals. Chicago newspapers would regularly denounce Parsons and called for his expulsion from the city.

As May 1 approached some employers granted a eight hour day or sometimes a nine hour day as a compromise. Across the nation 35,000 workers had received a shorter work day and 10,000 were on strike in April. On May 1 it is estimated that 200,000 went on strike through out the country. The movement was particularly strong in Chicago with 40,000 going on strike. Besides the Knights of Labor other organizations in the city supporting the strike included the Trade and Labor Assembly,

LABOR BATTLEGROUND

Central Labor Union, Eight Hour Association, and the International Working People's Association (IWPA). These groups individually and collectively had sponsored demonstrations during April which attracted between 20,000 and 25,000 people. The IWPA was founded by Parsons and August Spies. Some of the Chicago press attacked this pair on May 1. The *Chicago Mail* wrote:

There are two dangerous ruffians at large in this city; two sneaking cowards who are trying to create trouble. One of them is named Parsons; the other named Spies.

These two fellows have been at work fomenting disorder for the past ten years. They should have been driven out of the city long ago. They would not be tolerated in any other community on earth.

They have no love for the eight-hour movement, and are doing all they can to hamper it and prevent its success. These fellows do not want any reasonable concession. They are looking for riot and plunder. They haven't got one honest aim nor one honorable end in view.

Mark them for to-day. Keep them in view. Hold them personally responsible for any trouble that occurs. Make an example of them if trouble does occur.

Although Chicago was nervous as May 1, 1886 began, it was a peaceful day. The major event was a mass march down Michigan Avenue. This was led by Albert Parsons and 50,000 participated. The Trades and Labor Assembly ended the day with a huge ball.

On the first day of May the major strike occurring in Chicago was one which had started in February at the McCormick plant. This factory was located in the area of Western Avenue and Blue Island Street on both sides of the Chicago river. There had been labor problems at the plant for over a year. In early 1885 the workers struck for better pay. Pinkerton guards fired on a group of workers wounding one of them. The company owner, a horrified Mrs. McCormick, gave in and granted raises between 10 and 15 percent. A week after the strike Albert Parsons was making speeches a few blocks from the plant exhorting them to revolution. Parsons stated:

We are called by some communists, or socialists, or anarchists. We accept all three of the terms. We even accept the name of dynamiters. What is dynamite? It is the latest discovery of science by which power is placed in the hands of the weak and defenseless to protect them against the domination of others. Science says to the poor through the voice of dynamite: 'Be of good cheer, I will make you the equal of all other men'.

OPPOSITE PAGE

Police and strikers battle at McCormick Works on Western Avenue.

Parsons' paper the *Alarm* went even further:

> *One dynamite bomb, properly placed, will destroy a regiment. The revolutionist should experiment for himself. Especially should he practice throwing bombs.*

In this heated atmosphere trouble started again at McCormick works. In February, 1886 the Metalworker's section of the Knights of Labor asked the company to fire 5 non-union molders. A strike was threatened and McCormick shut the plant down. Two weeks later the harvester works was reopened with strikebreakers. In the meantime the eight-hour movement took hold in Chicago. On May 3, McCormick surprised everyone by granting ten hours pay for eight hours work to the employees at work in the plant. Of course union members on strike were left out of the agreement.

The Lumber Shovers' Union, on strike for shorter hours, had arranged for a rally the afternoon of the Third. The event was to be held in the vicinity of McCormick works. August Spies had been invited to speak. When he arrived almost 6,000 strikers had gathered. As he was finishing his speech the quitting bell rang at McCormick works. Although the Lumber Shovers' had nothing to do with the McCormick strike there were several hundred striking McCormick workers attending the rally. They charged the workers leaving the plant. The charging crowd threw stones at the strike-breakers causing them to flee back inside the plant. Initially there were few police present and they were unable to control the strikers. Windows were broken at the plant and there were shots fired from both the police and strikers. Shortly 200 police arrived on the scene and attacked the workers. The police using clubs and guns scattered the crowd. One striker was killed and 5 were seriously wounded. Six police were injured, three seriously, but none were shot.

August Spies was witness to some of the police action and saw many of the workers falling from police clubs and bullets. Another witness told Spies he had seen many workers killed by the police. Spies raced back to his paper, the *Arbeiter-Zeitung*, a socialist newspaper for German immigrant workers, to write an account of the rally. Spies also wrote a leaflet entitled "Revenge! Workingmen! To Arms!" which reported six workers had been killed. This misinformation had been also reported by the Chicago *Daily News* in a late night edition. Twenty Five Hundred copies of the "Revenge" flyer were printed and they were distributed that evening on the West Side and at labor meetings. This leaflet is reprinted on page 37.

Labor groups called for a protest rally to held the evening of May 4 in Haymarket Square. Haymarket Square was a area of Randolph street between Desplaines and Halsted streets. It was an area normally used to sell goods and farmer's produce. Adolph Fischer, a fellow member of the IWPA asked Spies to address the rally. Spies was shown a flyer which is reproduced on page 38. Spies demanded the phrase "Workingmen Arm Yourselves and Appear in Full Force!" be removed. He felt that the

REVENGE!

Workingmen, to Arms!!!

Your masters sent out their bloodhounds — the police —; they killed six of your brothers at McCormicks this afternoon. They killed the poor wretches, because they, like you, had the courage to disobey the supreme will of your bosses. They killed them, because they dared ask for the shortening of the hours of toil. They killed them to show you, "Free American Citizens!", that you must be satisfied and contended with whatever your bosses condescend to allow you, or you will get killed!

You have for years endured the most abject humiliations; you have for years suffered unmeasurable iniquities; you have worked yourself to death; you have endured the pangs of want and hunger; your Children you have sacrificed to the factory-lords — in short: You have been miserable and obedient slave all these years: Why? To satisfy the insatiable greed, to fill the coffers of your lazy thieving master? When you ask them now to lessen your burden, he sends his bloodhounds out to shoot you, kill you!

If you are men, if you are the sons of your grand sires, who have shed their blood to free you, then you will rise in your might, Hercules, and destroy the hideous monster that seeks to destroy you. To arms we call you, to arms!

Your Brothers.

Rache! Rache!

Arbeiter, zu den Waffen!

Arbeitendes Volk, heute Nachmittag mordeten die Bluthunde Eurer Ausbeuter 6 Eurer Brüder draußen bei McCormick's. Warum mordeten sie dieselben? Weil sie den Muth hatten, mit dem Loos unzufrieden zu sein, welches Eure Ausbeuter ihnen beschieden haben. Sie forderten Brod, man antwortete ihnen mit Blei, eingedenk der Thatsache, daß man damit das Volk am wirksamsten zum Schweigen bringen kann! Viele, viele Jahre habt Ihr alle Demüthigungen ohne Widerspruch ertragen, habt Euch vom frühen Morgen bis zum späten Abend geschunden, habt Entbehrungen jeder Art ertragen, habt Eure Kinder selbst geopfert — Alles, um die Schatzkammern Eurer Herren zu füllen, Alles für sie! Und jetzt, wo Ihr vor sie hintretet, und sie ersucht, Eure Bürde etwas zu erleichtern, da hetzen sie zum Dank für Eure Opfer ihre Bluthunde, die Polizei, auf Euch, um Euch mit Bleikugeln von der Unzufriedenheit zu kuriren Sklaven, wir fragen und beschwören Euch bei Allem, was Euch heilig und werth ist, rächt diesen scheußlichen Mord, den man heute an Euren Brüdern beging, und vielleicht morgen schon an Euch begehen wird. Arbeitendes Volk, Herkules, Du bist am Scheideweg angelangt. Wofür entscheidest Du Dich? Für Sklaverei und Hunger, oder für Freiheit und Brod? Entscheidest Du Dich für das Letztere, dann säume keinen Augenblick; dann, Volk, zu den Waffen! Vernichtung den menschlichen Bestien, die sich Deine Herrscher nennen! Rücksichtslose Vernichtung ihnen — das muß Deine Losung sein! Denk' der Helden, deren Blut den Weg zum Fortschritt, zur Freiheit und zur Menschlichkeit gebähnt — und strebe, ihre würdig zu werden!

Eure Brüder.

Attention Workingmen!

GREAT
MASS-MEETING

TO-NIGHT, at 7.30 o'clock,

AT THE

HAYMARKET, Randolph St., Bet. Desplaines and Halsted.

Good Speakers will be present to denounce the latest atrocious act of the police, the shooting of our fellow-workmen yesterday afternoon.

Workingmen Arm Yourselves and Appear in Full Force!

THE EXECUTIVE COMMITTEE.

Achtung, Arbeiter!

Große
Massen-Versammlung

Heute Abend, ½8 Uhr, auf dem

Heumarkt, Randolph-Straße, zwischen Desplaines- u. Halsted-Str.

☞ Gute Redner werden den neuesten Schurkenstreich der Polizei, indem sie gestern Nachmittag unsere Brüder erschoß, geißeln.

☞ Arbeiter, bewaffnet Euch und erscheint massenhaft!

Das Executiv-Comite.

phrase would be inflammatory. Fischer agreed but several hundred copies had already been distributed. A total of 20,000 flyers were passed out in the city.

Spies came to Haymarket Square that evening and found a small crowd milling about with no speakers. It was clearly disorganized. He mounted a truck wagon which was parked in front of the Crane Brothers factory on Desplaines just north of Randolph. A runner was sent to find Parsons and other speakers. A total of 1400 were present when Spies began to speak.

The Chicago Police Department had protested the rally but Mayor Carter Harrison had agreed to give it a permit. The Mayor did agree to keep 180 police lodged at the Desplaines stationhouse which was just a little more than a block from the rally. Mayor Harrison showed up as Spies was beginning to speak.

Spies commenting on the McCormick incident said:

It is said that I inspired the attack on McCormick's. That is a lie. The fight is going on. Now is the chance to strike for the existence of the oppressed classes. The oppressors want us to be content. They will kill us. The day is not far distant when we will resort to hanging these men. McCormick is the man who created the row Monday, and he must be held responsible for the murder of our brothers.

Spies talked for 20 minutes and then Parsons arrived. Parsons talked for 45 minutes. He stated:

Whenever you make a demand for an increase in pay, the militia and the deputy sheriff and the Pinkerton men are called out and you are shot and clubbed and murdered in the streets. I am not here for the purpose of inciting anybody, but to speak out, to tell the facts as they exist, even though it shall cost my life before morning. It behooves you, as you love your wife and children, if you don't want to see them perish with hunger, killed or cut down like dogs in the street, Americans, in the interest of your liberty and your independence, to arm, to arm yourselves.

When Parsons was almost finished Mayor Harrison left the rally and stopped at the Desplaines police station and told Captain Bonfield the speakers were coming to a close and he should release his men. The Mayor then rode his horse to his mansion 10 blocks away. The final speaker at the rally was Samuel Fielden. As he began to speak it started to rain and most of the crowd started to leave. There were only about 300 people left in the Square. Apparently Captain Bonfield became angry at some of the speaker's remarks which were reported to him. Without warning he sent his men from the station and up Desplaines to the speaker's site. Fielden stopped speaking and the crowd was taken by surprise. The police column marched to within 10 feet of the speakers wagon. Captain Ward announced, "In the name of the people of the State of Illinois, I command this meeting immediately and peaceably to disperse."

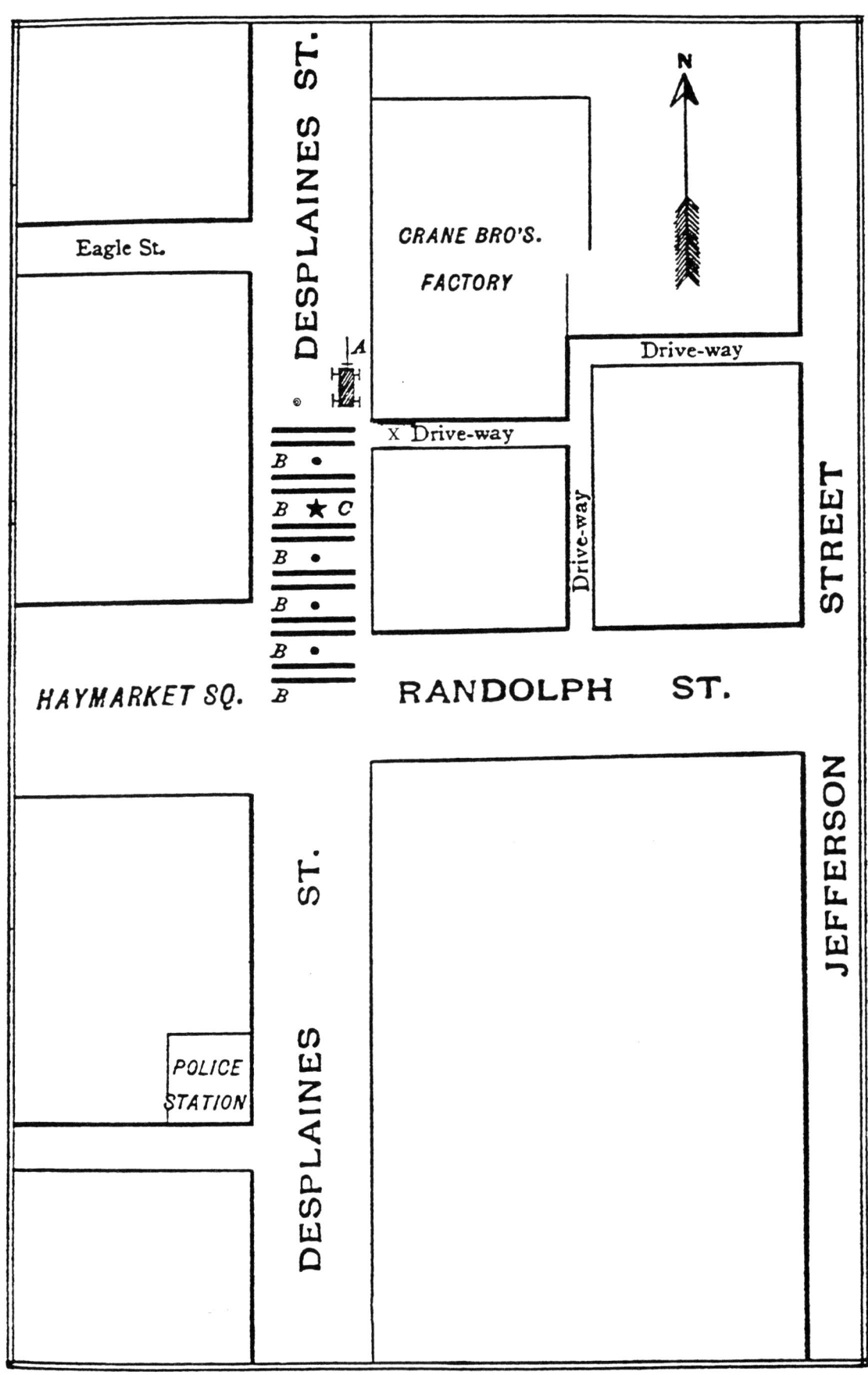

EXPLANATION OF THE MAP

A - The Speaker's Wagon   B - Six Companies of policemen
C - Where the Bomb exploded   ⊙ - Inspector Bonfield commanding police
X - Where bombthrower stood

Fielden started to step down from the wagon and stated, "We are peaceable."

At this point someone standing in the alley just south of Crane Brothers threw the first dynamite bomb in U.S. history. The bomb landed in the middle of the police column killing one officer instantly. Over 70 were injured. In the next six weeks another six policemen died of their wounds. A seventh died a few years later.

The inflamed police quickly regrouped and attacked the remaining crowd. They fired at spectators and charged them with clubs. One in the crowd was known to be killed and 12 wounded. More are suspected of being killed or dying of wounds but their bodies were buried secretly.

In the next few days police raided several dozen socialist and anarchist gathering places as well as a private home. Eventually 200 people were arrested and held to get information. Newspapers, business leaders and even labor unions demanded action to stop anarchy. The Grand Jury indited 31 on various conspiracy charges with 10 indited for murder. These 10 were charged with being accessories before the fact to the murder of Policeman Mathias Degan. Later as other policemen died their names were added to the charges. Of the ten eight were actually tried. They were Parsons, Spies, Fielden, Michael Schwab, Adolph Fischer, George Engel, Louis Lingg, and Oscar Neebe. William Seliger became a witness for the state and he received immunity. The suspected bomb thrower Rudolph Schnaubelt was briefly held, released and then never found again.

The Illinois law which was applied in the Haymarket case stated:

An accessory is one who stands by, and aids, abets, or assists, or who, not being present aiding, abetting, or assisting, hath advised, encouraged, aided or abetted the perpetration of the crime. He who thus aids, abets, advises or encourages, shall be considered as principal and punished accordingly.
Every such accessory may be indicted and convicted at the same time as the principal or before or after his conviction, and whether principal is convicted or amendable to justice or not, and punished as principal.

Six weeks after the bomb the trial started. From the beginning it was known there would be a guilty verdict. State's Attorney Grinnell told the jury he would name the bomb-thrower but never did so. At the end of the trial Grinnell stated that it was enough that the defendants advocated violence and since people died as a result then a guilty verdict was justified. Judge Joseph Gary did not hesitate to show his bias. He gave great latitude to the prosecution, limited the defense and told the jury that failure to convict would put the nation at risk.

On June 20, 1886 the verdict was given and all were sentenced to hang except Neebe who received 15 years. Judge Gary stated, "Whoever advises murder is

SCENE OF HAYMARKET EXPLOSION

This 1886 illustration represents the north side of Randolph street, where it is intersected by Desplaines. The prominent building on the right is Bryan Wadden's saloon, facing Randolph street. An alley separates it from Crane Brothers factory which is the building with the many chimneys whose corner is seen in the center of the picture. Just north of this alley, on Desplaines street, stood the wagon from which the speeches were delivered.

OPPOSITE PAGE

The Moment of the Haymarket explosion at Randolph and Desplaines.

himself guilty of the murder that is committed pursuant to his advice". The Illinois Supreme Court agreed with this ruling. The trial created a firestorm of protest in the nation and even the world. Three of the eight were not even at Haymarket Square and the prosecution was unable to prove that the incident was inspired by the preaching of the anarchists. Some business leaders in Chicago felt that executions would create martyrs for the cause of revolution.

Thousands began to petition Governor Oglesby both for and against pardons. Then on November 6, 1887, when pressure was at the highest, four dynamite bombs were found in the cell of Louis Lingg. This put a damper on the pardon movement. Nevertheless at a hearing on November 9 the governor was handed petitions with 200,000 signatures. These were not only from Chicago but New York and elsewhere around the world. Samuel Gompers, President of the American Federation of Labor, plead for the executions to be commuted.

On the morning before the executions Lingg blew half his head away with a dynamite cap which had been smuggled into his cell. Later that day the Governor commuted the scheduled execution for Fielden and Schwab. The following day, November 11th, the remaining four, Parsons, Spies, Fischer and Engel were hung.

The executions did not stop the case. The controversy was revived in early 1892 when the Chicago police raided socialist meeting places. This was due to large amounts of money which had been raised for the police by Chicago businessmen to fight radicalism. A group known as the Citizens Association had raised almost $500,000 for use by the police in fighting radicals. Captain Bonfield came under investigation for corruption and was suspended from the force. At the same time a business group funded a police monument to be placed at the site of the bomb. This statute of a policeman stayed at the site until the 1970s when it was removed to the Police Academy because of continuing vandalism. The base of this statute can still be seen at Randolph and the Kennedy Expressway.

When John Altgeld was elected Governor in November, 1892 pressure was put on him by his friend and law partner Clarence Darrow to release the three remaining defendants from prison. Altgeld told Darrow:

If I conclude to pardon those men, it will not meet with the approval you expect. Let me tell you - from that day, I will be a dead man.

Judge Gary, now being criticized with the attention on the case, wrote a magazine article in early 1893 blasting the defendants. He also attacked the defense attorney and said that labor organizations were agents of revolution. On June 26, 1893 Governor Altgeld delivered his pardon message. This was the day after the Haymarket Monument was dedicated at the gravesite of the executed men in Forest Park twelve miles west of downtown Chicago. This is shown on page 45. Governor Altgeld

This is an illustration of the Haymarket Monument which is the gravesite to seven of the eight men tried as a result of the Haymarket explosion. The monument is located in Forest Home Cemetery in Forest Park, Illinois. The monument was originally built and maintained by the Pioneer Aid and Support Association. It was later deeded to the Illinois Labor History Society and the above zinc cut illustration is in their collection.

wrote that he could not agree with Judge Gary's ruling that the State did not have to identify the bomb-thrower or even prove that he came under the influence of the defendants. Altgeld wrote, "In all the centuries during which government has been maintained among men and crime has been punished, no judge in a civilized country has ever laid down such a rule before". Altgeld also stated that Judge Gary was shown to be prejudiced by the trial record. Altgeld gave an absolute pardon to Schwab, Fielden and Neebe and they were released that day.

The next morning the *Tribune* denounced the German-born Altgeld's decision. It editorialized:

It was generally understood that the anarchists were to be let go in the event of Altgeld's election. The anarchists believed that he was not merely an alien by birth, but an alien by temperament and sympathies, and they were right. He has apparently not a drop of true American blood in his veins. He does not reason like an American, nor feel like one, and consequently he does not behave like one.

Altgeld was thrown from office in 1896 and finished his life as a law partner with Clarence Darrow. Haymarket became a significant labor holiday through out much of the world. In 1889 the International Labor Congress, meeting in Paris, voted to make May 1 a memorial to the "Chicago Martyrs". In many countries May 1st is treated similarly to Labor Day in the U.S.

Another aftereffect of Haymarket was the establishment of Fort Sheridan. The Commercial Club of Chicago feared Haymarket was not a one-time event but part of a revolutionary strategy. They offered to give the government 600 acres of land along Lake Michigan 25 miles north of the city for the establishment of a military base. On March 3, 1887 the government accepted the offer and the army base was founded. Sheridan Road was built for the use of troops to travel from the base to Chicago. Ultimately many wealthy individuals moved to the North Shore area for the protection the base provided. Businessmen also provided funds for the navy to establish the Great Lakes Naval Station north of Chicago.

On March 25, 1992 the Chicago City Council voted to grant historic-landmark status to the one block of Desplaines between Lake and Randolph. To date, however, the area, which stands for the eight-hour day worldwide, has no memorial or designation.

REFORM

AND EARLY

TRADE UNION

BATTLES

3

HULL-HOUSE AND PULLMAN (1894)

After the Haymarket episode a movement began in Chicago to reform conditions of immigrant workers. This was a reaction to the violence of Haymarket and a belief that the "revolution" favored by the anarchists and socialists was not possible.
Jane Addams, the daughter of a influential state Senator, was to become the standard-bearer of this movement in Chicago.

After graduation from college in 1882 she traveled for most of the next seven years in Europe. She saw the terrible slums of East London and visited the Toynbee Hall settlement house. There she discovered how a person from a privileged background could work on social problems. Arnold Toynbee had started a movement where privileged and educated people would settle in the slums to cure social evils. The social reformers not only wanted to decrease poverty but enlighten the lives of the poor with literature, classes, theater, art, and music.

Addams brought the settlement ideas back to Chicago and moved into the Hull mansion at Polk and Halsted streets. Hull was a millionaire who had died recently. His mansion which was in a neighborhood which had changed from wealthy to one of poor immigrants by the 1880s was given to Addams by the executors of the Hull estate. Together with Ellen Gates Starr she formed the Hull-House settlement house in September, 1889. The neighborhood was populated by immigrants from Italy, Russia, Greece, Poland, Ireland, France, China, Netherlands, Germany, and Africa.

Hull-House residents threw themselves into labor issues. Jane Addams was opposed to radical ideology but she never tired of attacking the sweatshops which so many of the West Side poor worked in. In 1893, after an investigation of the sweatshop system by Hull-House's Florence Kelly, Governor Altgeld pushed the Illinois legislature into passing the strongest anti-sweatshop law in the nation. Kelly was appointed by Governor Altgeld to be the first Chief Factory Inspector of Illinois. She used this position to promote factory safety issues in the state. Other safety issues were also

Jane Addams' Hull-House Museum
The University of Illinois at Chicago

The Jane Addams' Hull-House Museum, owned and operated by the University of Illinois at Chicago, is an historic site and memorial to Jane Addams, her innovative settlement house programs and associates, and the neighborhood they served. Restored by the University of Illinois in the mid-1960s, this two-building complex was declared a National Historic Landmark in 1967 and a Chicago Landmark in 1974.

The Hull Mansion, pictured above, was originally built as a country home in 1856. Occupied by Jane Addams in 1889, it served as the nucleus for the thirteen–building settlement house complex that grew around it in subsequent years. The interior of this building, where Jane Addams and Ellen Gates Starr began their world famous social settlement, has been restored to look as it did in the early days of Hull-House. Original furnishings, paintings, memorabilia, photographs, and rotating exhibits recreate the history of the settlement and the work of its residents.

Next door is the Residents' Dining Hall, added to Hull-House in 1905. On the first floor is an extensive exhibit on the history of the surrounding University neighborhood as it appeared around the turn of the century. This exhibit is laid out to correspond to the geography of the area itself and is part of an ongoing project to present and interpret materials on the history of an important urban community.

The Jane Addams' Hull-House Museum is open to the public for tours weekdays 10 a.m. to 4 p.m. and, during the summer only, on Sundays from noon to 5 p.m. An introductory slide program is available to drop-in visitors in conjunction with the tours. Speical programs on topics relating to the history of Hull-House and the neighborhood are also available to groups making reservations in advance.

The Jane Addams' Hull-House Museum is located at the corner of Polk and Halsted streets, on the campus of the University of Illinois at Chicago. Admission is free. Parking is available in a University lot across the street. For more information call 413-5353.

taken up by the settlement residents. After Louise De Koven Bowen, descendent of one of the original settlers at Fort Dearborn, found out about the enormous rate of tuberculosis at the Pullman plant, she embarrassed the management into making corrections. Jane Addams tried to mediate the Pullman strike but met with failure and anger from both sides.

Two years after Hull-House opened Addams supported a shirtmakers strike protesting wage cuts. The settlement houses were almost always involved in local strikes. Some of these were failures such as Addams attempt to arbitrate the Pullman strike. Hull-House played an important role in organizing women's trade unions, among them a book binders' union, a shoemakers' and a shirt and cloak-makers' union. The residents were successful in initiating legislation curtailing child labor and long work hours. In the next century Hull-House continued it's effort with labor issues with the clothing workers and others.

A financial panic hit the nation beginning in 1893. The recession did not affect Chicago immediately because of construction of the Columbian Exposition World's Fair of 1893. After the fair ended layoffs and wage cuts came. The railroad industry was no exception.

George Pullman came to Chicago in 1859 and made a reputation with his engineering skills of raising buildings to meet new street heights. Later he designed the luxury Pullman sleeper railroad cars which took many of the bumps out of rail travel. In 1880 Pullman decided to build a model factory town nine miles south of the Chicago city limits (then 47th Street). Pullman had decided that Chicago had too many bad influences such as liquor and radicalism. He bought 600 acres of land next to Lake Calumet. Pullman felt there would be an increase of 10 percent efficiency in the workforce because of the natural air conditioning of the lake.

The town of Pullman was located between what is now 103rd Street on the north, 115th Street on the South, Cottage Grove Avenue on the West and the Calumet Expressway on the East. The factory was located in the center with two residential areas on either side. Pullman contained all the housing necessary for both workers and management. The type of housing was assigned by rank. The top executives got the biggest houses and unskilled workers lived in small apartments. Taverns were not allowed in the town. Pullman contained the stores, shops, schools, and recreational facilities which Pullman thought the workforce needed. One church was built for use by all denominations. Rents and store debts were deducted from the employee paychecks. The town of Pullman had a reputation of a model town and people from around the world came to see it. What was not seen was Pullman's attempts to gouge his employees. He bought water from the city of Chicago at five cents a thousand gallons and sold it to employees at ten cents a thousand. Pullman bought gas at 33 cents per thousand feet and sold it to employees for $2.25 a thousand!

The Streets of Chicago

When the Panic of 1893 struck Eugene Victor Debs was secretary of the Brotherhood of Locomotive Firemen. This was a conservative craft railway union and Debs was dissatisfied with their philosophy. He called for a meeting in Chicago in June, 1893. At this meeting the American Railway Union (ARU) was founded. The ARU would include all railroad occupations. The lowest paid and unskilled such as track walkers, section hands, and engine wipers had never been organized. In the spring of 1894 Deb's ARU shut down the Great Northern and won most of their demands. This victory gave the new union prestige and a membership gain to almost 150,000 members.

The financial recession of 1893 caused travel to plunge and Pullman fired 2200 workers from the Pullman company while reducing wages 25 percent for most of those left. Together with the cutting of work hours this resulted in a 50 percent reduction in earnings for most. At the same time he refused to lower the employees' rents which were already 25 percent higher than similar housing in Chicago. Many of the workers only had a few cents left in their paychecks after the deductions.

The Pullman workers began to join Deb's ARU in mass. By May, 1894 almost all 3000 of the workers at Pullman were members. The Pullman local hoped that if a strike were called the rest of the union would refuse to handle trains that were using Pullman cars. Clarence Darrow, who the year before had been a leader in the Haymarket pardons and was now an attorney for the North Western Railroad, decided to join Debs and become the attorney for the union.

On May 9, 1894 a committee, elected by the workers, met with Pullman to discuss the wage cuts and rents. Pullman said his workers were his "children" and they were lucky to have any work at all. Pullman promptly fired all those on the committee and ordered them thrown out of their homes. On May 11 3000 workers at Pullman walked off their jobs. Debs would not call for a boycott fearing a legal attack from the courts. On June 9 the American Railway Union met in Chicago with delegates representing 465 local chapters. On June 20 a Pullman sempstress, Jennie Curtis, appeared before the delegates and told a story of eviction on the day of her father's funeral with demands for back rent. This inflamed the delegates and they overruled Deb's caution and voted to boycott all trains which had Pullman cars.

On June 26 the boycott began and men who refused to handle Pullman cars were fired by their respective companies. Strikes started at railway depots across the country. Farm products including meat began to run short in most cities of the country. The joint railway companies, known as the General Managers Association (GMA), welcomed the fight with the union. They had been dismayed by the early victory by Debs with the Great Northern Railway. The GMA knew federal judges disliked boycotts specifically and unions generally. The GMA began putting Pullman cars on trains which never had them before and with trains which carried the mail. The GMA recruited 125,000 strikebreakers and guards.

Once mail began to be affected a federal judge issued an injunction on July 2. Troops were called from Fort Sheridan to enter Chicago and protect the trains. President Cleveland issued a statement which said:

If it takes the entire Army and Navy to deliver a postcard in Chicago, that card will be delivered, -- Free!

When the 15,000 troops marched into Chicago on July 3rd there had been no violence or serious trouble in Chicago. Governor Altgeld had not asked for the troops and sent a telegram in protest. It stated:

Waiving all questions of courtesy, I will see that the State of Illinois is able to take care of itself. Our military force is ample. To ignore a local government, when the local government is ready and able to enforce the law, not only insults the people of this state by imputing to them an inability to govern themselves, but it is a violation of a basic principle of our institutions. I ask the immediate withdrawal of the Federal troops from active duty in this state.

The appearance of federal troops inflamed the workers and ordinary citizens of Chicago. On July 5 much of what remained of the Columbian Exposition buildings burned in Jackson Park. The only building that remained was what is now the Museum of Science and Industry. The stockyards had been shut down by the rail strike and federal troops attempted to clear the tracks. Five thousand rioters controlled the area and the troops were forced to withdraw. The following day over 700 railroad cars were destroyed in the Fiftieth Street Yards by fire. The roaming crowd started at 3 o'clock and did not stop until 10 o'clock. This created a wall of fire a mile and half long. Not a car, switch tower, signal post or tool shanty was left standing. Many of the cars were full of anthracite coal, and as the woodwork burned away great piles of coal dumped on the tracks. These piles burned on for days. The tremendous heat twisted the tracks destroyed them.

On July 6 troops fired on civilians at railway yards at 47th and Ashland. Twenty were killed or wounded by bayonets and gunshot. Within two days a modern equivalent of tens of millions of dollars of property were destroyed. Cars at yards were overturned and burned. For two nights the South Side had a red glow from the flames. Troops killed 13 men and women by the end of the strike. Three soldiers were blown up when their artillery carriage detonated.

On the seventh of July Debs and other ARU officials were arrested and charged with criminal conspiracy. The arrests effectively left the strike leaderless and demoralized. On July 12 a meeting of the American Federation of Labor rejected a call for help. The ARU then attempted to call off the strike if workers would not be discriminated against in rehiring. This was rejected by Pullman. July 18 Pullman announced the plant would be opened to those who would agree to never join a union while working

MAP SHOWING LOCALITY WHERE THE MILITIA FIRED ON THE STRIKERS.

MILITIAMEN FIRE INTO THE MOB AT LOOMIS AND FORTY-NINTH STREETS.

SPECIAL OFFICER STARK SHOOTS TWO STRIKERS AT 113TH STREET.

MOB SETTING FIRE TO ILLINOIS CENTRAL FREIGHT CARS.

POLICE FIRE ON THE STRIKERS AT THE FORT WAYNE TRACKS.

WRECKED FREIGHT CARS AND ENGINE NEAR 104TH STREET.

The Streets of Chicago

at Pullman. On August 2, 1894 the Pullman plant reopened. All ARU men wishing to reapply had to surrender their membership cards. Some of the leaders were blacklisted. Debs was sentenced to six months for contempt and served his term in the jail in Woodstock.

Even in victory George Pullman continued contempt for his workers. As the winter approached Governor Altgeld appealed to Pullman for a contribution for many of his former workers. Almost 2000 were jobless and destitute. The Governor took a tour of the Pullman area and found 6000 people starving, 80 percent of them women and children. Altgeld asked Pullman to suspend rents, and cut work hours in half so more could be employed. Pullman rejected all pleas. Altgeld had to ask the citizens of Illinois for contributions to solve the crisis. Cook County had flour and rice distributed to the Pullman residents. When Pullman died in 1897 his family had the coffin covered in asphalt, steel rails, and concrete to protect the site from vandalism.

Although the strike permanently ended the American Railway Union, Eugene Debs decided America's workers needed political direction. He became the Socialist Party candidate for President five times, winning almost one million votes in 1912. Clarence Darrow, the ARU's attorney, went on to be a great labor lawyer and crusader for unpopular ideas. He argued the cause of evolution in the Scopes Monkey Trial. There were other ramifications of the strike. Governor John Altgeld, angry at President Cleveland's use of troops in Chicago, led the opposition to his renomination at the 1896 Convention held in Chicago. William Jennings Bryan made his famous "Cross of Gold" speech at the convention and took on the populist cause of the workingman who was being crucified by the monopolies and tight money. This important speech is reprinted as Appendix B-3. Bryan, with Altgeld's help, was nominated. Both Bryan and Altgeld were defeated in the November elections. Finally in 1898 the Illinois Supreme Court ordered the an end to the Pullman experiment. The ruled that Pullman was "incompatible with the theory and spirit of our institutions".

TEAMSTERS (1902)

The first major labor battle of the Twentieth century was local and occurred in 1902. Major Nineteenth century labor fights in Chicago were usually part of a national issue. The Great Strike of 1877, Haymarket, and Pullman were part of national movements or strikes.

On July 7, 1902 the Freight Handlers' Union struck 24 railroad companies. Over 9000 men walked out. The strike was for an 18 percent wage increase and union recognition. The Freight Handlers sought help from other unions, primarily the Teamsters. The Teamsters were the men which drove the freight to the merchants in Chicago. The National Teamsters tried to ignore the strike because the Freight Handlers had gone on strike without the permission of the Chicago Federation of

Labor. The railroad imported strikebreakers and former employees to break the strike. The Chicago Teamsters, defying their national leaders, and with 25,000 members threatened a general strike. The State Board of Arbitration attempted to settle the issue but the Chicago Teamsters finally struck on July 12. The next day the local Teamsters announced they would not handle any freight going to or from the railroads. The strike spread to the Longshoremen of the steamship lines who dropped their freight and walked out also.

Trucks thoughout the city were attacked by crowds of up to 3000 strikers and sympathizers. The supply of meat and other goods became short. On July 15 the national President of the Teamsters, Albert Young, ordered the Teamsters back to work. President Curran of the Freight Handlers ordered the strike ended on July 16th for the wage increase the companies had offered. Curran said the strike was called off, because though the local rank and file was with them to a man, the national Teamsters had turned them down. He did not want to see the local Freight Handlers or local Teamsters demoralized. Curran stated:

There is one lesson to be learned from the strike and that is that no representative body should agree not to engage in a sympathetic strike where the principles of unionism are directly involved. That was the case with the teamsters. In my opinion the arbitration agreement between them and the team owners should be altered and the power withdrawn from the executive board of their organization to make such agreements without being first approved by the members at large.

TEAMSTERS (1905)

The Teamsters strike of 1905 was the first pitched battle between organized labor and employers organized in the form of an employer association. The resources of the national organizations of Teamsters pitted against the Employers Association of Chicago. This battle ended up with 25 dead, 415 injured, and a cost of millions of dollars spent in an aggressive offense and defense by the two sides. To that point, the Teamsters strike was the most serious industrial upheaval that Chicago had seen, with the possible exception of Pullman.

This fight began in November 1904, with the United Garment Workers union and the association of wholesale-tailors which had 28 firms as members. The parties met to discuss contracts. The employers wanted an open shop which would not require union membership. The garment workers wanted a union shop and wanted grievances arbitrated. The employers refused these demands. Several thousand workers walked out. As the strike progressed many of the garment workers returned to work under a "open shop". The cutters and some of the more skilled craftsmen remained faithful to their union. They tried to get assistance from other labor organizations in the city.

Teamsters overturned delivery wagons through out the city in the 1902 strike (CHS).

LABOR BATTLEGROUND

The teamsters were urged to lend their help because of their control of the streets. The efforts to persuade the drivers to refuse to work for the large clothing makers failed because the teamsters had contracts. Then the large mail order houses were targeted. These employers had few garment workers but they were targets for pressure because of the large number of drivers they employed and prompt shipments were part of their business policy. On April 6, 1905 Montgomery Ward was asked to fire their 20 non union garment workers and the company refused. The company's 71 teamsters then went out in an sympathetic strike.

Clashes with the police came immediately. Montgomery Ward sent out shipments of merchandise and the trucks were attacked. Streets were blocked in several areas of the city and wagons were abandoned as their drivers were attacked. Under the leadership of John G. Shedd, of Marshall Field, the employers then devised a strikebreaking tactic and formed the Employers' Teaming company. This company was made up of 28 of the biggest business houses and it would have 100 wagons to deliver goods. On April 20 Shedd sent for the notorious James Farley. Farley was an infamous strikebreaker who had not hesitated to kill strikers in Boston and Pittsburgh.

Within a few days the garment workers decided they had nothing to gain from this battle and called off their strike. The International President of the Teamsters canceled the strike on April 24. Montgomery Ward refused to rehire the teamsters who had struck the company. Three days later the Teamsters then restarted the strike and 3000 teamsters walked out in the city. Those employed by the State street department stores, several of the wholesale stores, all of the express companies, and several teaming companies struck. April 29 saw a major riot in what was known as the "Little Hell" district in the area of Crosby & Hobbie. An Employer Association barn was raided and destroyed. A non-union driver was attacked and killed. On May 1 Farley and fellow strikebreaker Frank Curry arrived. The immediately set out to import 900 strikebreakers, mainly black (see *Tribune* cartoon on page 63). The next day non-union drivers were attacked all over the city. Stones and other missiles rained down on the wagons. Police were helpless to stop the violence. Two were killed and 110 injured. Fighting over the next few days quickly escalated to shooting between the two sides. Curry, one of the strikebreaker leaders lost an eye at Lake Street and Michigan Avenue when a bottle was dropped from a building. Governor Deneen refused a request by Montgomery Ward to call the state militia to Chicago. He said he would not do so without a request from the mayor. Even school children took part in the battle when students walked out of Carter Harrison school over non-union delivery of coal.

On May 28 the employers were able to secure a federal injunction against union interference with non-union wagons, barns or premises. President Shea of the International Teamsters, President Dold of the Chicago Federation of Labor and ten other union officials were indicted the next day on the charge of conspiracy to prevent deliveries. During the third week of May President Samuel Gompers of the American

Newspapers played up racial attitudes of the day during strikes.

The police break a Teamster blockade in 1905 strike.

PUBLIC NOTICE!

All friends and customers in nearby towns and States, outside of Chicago and Cook County, are hereby informed that we are making shipments in all departments with our usual promptness.

The efforts of striking teamsters to boycott and blockade our establishment have signally failed.

We have cleared up all delayed orders, and are receiving and shipping goods by mail, express and freight, just as usual, and shall continue so to do.

Orders can be sent us with full assurance of immediate and careful filling and dispatching.

Our stock of merchandise is the largest and best assorted we have ever had, and we will please you in every particular—or "your money back." Safe delivery guaranteed.

Catalogue Coupon.
If you live outside of Chicago and Cook Co. and have not our latest Catalogue No. 73, over 1,100 pages, send for one today. No Charge.

Name _____
P. O. _____
R. F. D. _____ County _____ State _____

If you are interested in knowing the causes and history of this, the most foolish strike that union dictators ever inflicted upon an unsuspecting public, ask us, providing you reside outside of Chicago and Cook County, to mail you our strike circular.

MONTGOMERY WARD & CO.
Michigan Av., Madison and Washington Sts., CHICAGO.

Advertisement placed by Montgomery Ward during the 1905 strike.

Street Riots Are Features of Big Sympathetic Strike of Teamsters.

GOING WEST OVER WASHINGTON ST BRIDGE

Police had to escort wagons through blockades and around the city.

FULTON AND JEFFERSON BLOCKADE

Industrial Workers of the World (IWW) Organization Chart.

The Streets of Chicago

Federation of Labor came to Chicago to try and make peace. This attempt resulted in failure when the railway express companies refused to rehire their drivers.

In June charges of bribery of some of the union officials surfaced. John Driscall, secretary of the Chicago Coal Team Owners Association, stated he had intervened in over 400 strikes. He said he spent $50,000 bribing teamster officials to stay out of strikes or to break them. The grand jury began to investigate many of the unions in Chicago. On July 1 the grand jury indicted 54 union leaders and employer representatives. Gradually the life was being taken from the strike. The strike funds were depleted by July 1. Men were drifting back to work and slowly police protection was withdrawn from the wagons. The Teamsters union voted to end the strike after 105 days on July 20, 1905.

In this first test of the sympathy strike the labor unions could not match the tremendous resources of the Chicago business community. Ironically in the midst of this battle a convention took place on June 27, 1905 in Brand's Hall located at Clark and Erie. This was the founding convention of the Industrial Workers of the World (IWW). Present were leaders Big Bill Haywood, Eugene Debs, Mother Jones, and Lucy Parsons. Their goal was to organize all workers into 'One Big Union' (see chart on the next page). The IWW felt the American Federation of Labor would only organize skilled craft workers. This convention felt the AFL was too tied into the economic system and too conservative. Chicago's location in the center of the country made it a natural home for this organization. Although this organization was too extreme to attract much of a following in Chicago, it did play an important role in Western states and industries. Later John L. Lewis would use some of the IWW's theory to organize his C.I.O. among unskilled industrial workers.

STREETCAR STRIKE (1903)

Chicago's streetcar workers had two important strikes in this pre-World War I period. The first was in 1885. The second battle in 1903 was of lasting importance. This strike in 1903 resulted in the union recognition with no discrimination. There was no wage increase. Both walkouts involved disputes over higher wages, recognition of the union, and discrimination against union men.

The first strike in 1885 was described in Chapter 2. That strike involved the horse car days of Charles T. Yerkes. Men on Yerkes west side lines struck for higher pay, recognition of the union and better working conditions. Men on the north side struck in sympathy. About 1500 men were involved. This was prior to the organization of the Amalgamated Association of Street and Electric Employees of America.

The second strike involved 3000 men on the south side lines in 1903. The strike was called in November and lasted 13 days. The entire system of the Chicago City railway

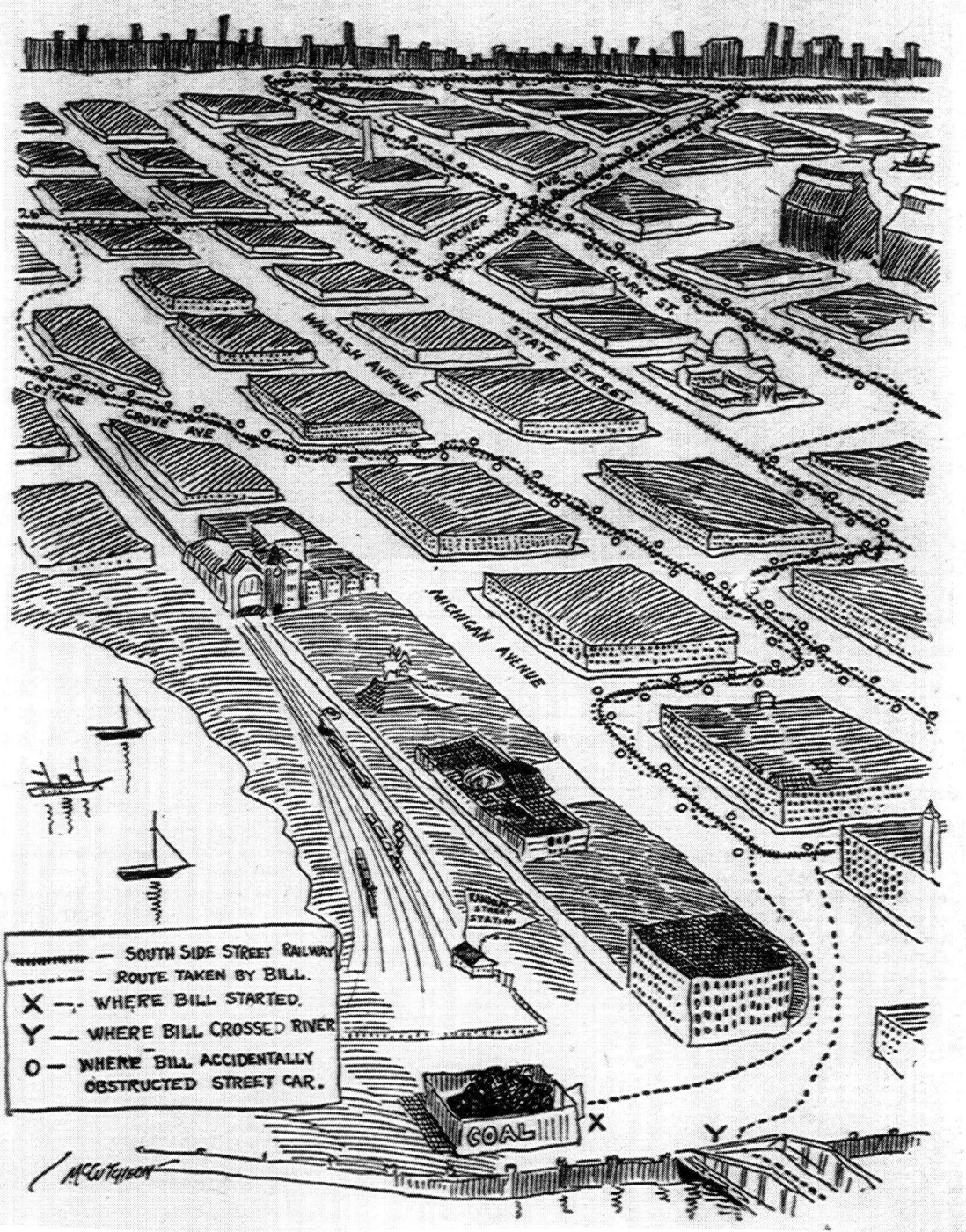

Newspaper cartoon of the Streetcar strike of 1903.

was paralyzed for more than one week. Professional strikebreakers and gunmen were imported to man the cars and much rioting occurred.

After the strike vote on November 6, 1903 the companies secured contracts with the firemen and teamsters for a one year period. This would ensure continued operation of their power plants. The streetcar companies hired James "Boss" Farley who had a long record of breaking street car strikes. He had 500 men who worked for him. He would show up in Chicago two years later when the Teamster struck. Farley had been in many other cities such as Cleveland, St. Louis, and Brooklyn. His body carried two bullets from past strikes.

The south side lines carried 750,000 commuters over 320 miles of track. When the strike started many members of the public wore support buttons which said "Stand for Principle, I Will Walk". The main issues were a wage increase, union recognition and an end to discrimination against union members. On the second day an attempt was made on the Wentworth line to move cars from 23rd street to the Loop. Police were on board all of the cars as well as lining the route. In spite of these precautions several cars were wrecked and two men were killed and 11 injured in the fighting. Coal cars were overturned and used as barricades. Conductors on cars were dragged off and crews were beaten. Officials of the company charged union leaders with instigating attacks on the cars. The strike leaders said the rioting was due to the irresponsible conduct of the imported strikebreakers and gunmen.

The next day the brother of the President of the union, W.D. Mahon, was clubbed and mortally wounded by a crowd which included his brother. He had taken the first car out at the barns at 77th & Vincennes. Riots greeted the cars when they arrived downtown at Clark & Van Buren. The Teamsters joined the battle and used their horses and delivery wagons to block car routes in the Loop.

The police guard was increased to over 1000. On the third day the companies put the strike breakers into the car barns which became barracks. The police increased their role to start collecting fares and managing other business affairs of the companies. The key to the strike became the Teamster's help in blocking cars and stopping the delivery of coal to the power plants. On the fourth day the car barn at 39th and Wentworth was invaded with the strikebreakers beaten and their bedding burned. The police increased their force to 1300 and decided to run both the Cottage Grove cable system as well as the Wentworth electric system.

Clarence Darrow took an active role in the strike attempting to negotiate for the strikers and condemning both Mayor Carter Harrison and the use of police. The biggest riot of the strike took place on November 22 when a supply wagon for the strikebreakers left company headquarters at 2020 State Street. The police and the crowds attacked each other at Archer and Throop where several died. Darrow was able to negotiate an end to the strike on November 25. The union was recognized and the companies pledged non-discrimination. There was no wage increase.

MEATPACKERS STRIKE (1904)

The Stock Yards was a square mile area of meatpacking companies which was bordered by Ashland on the west, Halsted on the east, 39th Street on the north, and 47th Street on the south. This was a major industry in Chicago employing 20,000 butchers and 15,000 oilers. Meatpackers handled daily 25,000 cattle, 46,000 hogs, and 20,000 sheep. This resulted in total daily income of several million dollars for the packers. The meatpackers strike was the first important battle in this industry, it was violent, resulting in little gain for the union.

The basic issues for the union, the Amalgamated Meat Cutters and Butcher Workmen, were wages, shorter hours, and union recognition. The union wanted the same pay and working conditions in all the packing centers. Some of the packing plants paid the men much more that others. The companies felt that most of the workers were unskilled and should not participate in a trade agreement. The union also wanted women fired to give places for men in the slaughtering departments. On May 28, 1904 the old agreement expired and negotiations began for a new contract. On July 12 a strike was called in all plants controlled by Chicago packers in Chicago and several other cities. This involved 50,000 men through out U.S. but was centered in Chicago. Another 50,000 were idled as a result. Seven major companies were involved, with Swift and Armour the two biggest. The companies rejected a wage increase but offered arbitration which the union rejected.

As the strike began crowds of strikers gathered at intersections in the Stock Yard area. At 47th and Ashland meat wagons were attacked and turned over. Hundreds were at 45th and Paulina when the police opened fire and wounded seven. Streetcars carrying strikebreakers, who were mainly black, were stoned by strikers. By July 16th the union agreed to arbitration because of the strikebreakers. The union also decided to open and operate their own plant called Cooperative Packing Plant at 1630 W. 47th Street. A tentative strike settlement was made on July 21. The settlement called for wages and working conditions to be arbitrated with strikers to be called back within 45 days.

Almost as soon as the agreement was signed it fell apart. The Packers said their was no guarantee strikers would be called back. They said that part of agreement only applied to discrimination cases. That night a mob of 5000 stoned three electric cars taking 200 blacks from the plant at 45th and Union. Two days later mobs attacked blacks coming into the plant at 35th and Halsted. Many were severely beaten. Agents for the Packers were going through the Deep South recruiting blacks to come north to act as strikebreakers. July 24, 94 trains arrived in Chicago, filled with black

NOTICE!
WE CAN WIN IF WE STAND BY THE UNION.

If we obey the Unions Rules to molest no person or property and abide strictly by the laws of the Country. All men on strike should retire to their homes and attend their various Union Meetings for all information. If you follow the above instructions you will be of great assistance in helping to win this strike.

Your organization will not assist you if you get into unlawful trouble.

AMALGAMATED MEAT CUTTERS & BUTCHER WORKMEN OF N. A.

Notice

Jedes Mitglied den A. M. C. & B. W. of N. A. ist hiermit aufgefordert sich von allen Gewaltthätigkeiten, Aufruhr und s. w. fernzuhalten und nur die Extra Versammlungen der Local zu derer es angehört zu besuchen, wo jeder Mann seine Instruktion erhält und über alle Verhandlungen mit den Packers Auskunt ertheilt wird. Nur wenn abrige Befehle erfüllt werden und und als gute Bürger Bürger auftuhren wird der Kampf gewonnen. Alf thut eure Schuldigkeit als gute Union Mitglieder und Bürger.

VYHLÁŠKA.

Můžeme vyhráti, když budeme státi při unii.

Když uposlechneme nařízení unie neobtěžovati žádné osoby, neničiti majetky a přísně zachovati zákony a pravidla této země. Všichni muži stávkující nechť jsou ve svých domovech a pro informace do schůze unie přijdou. Vaše unie vám nemůže pomoci, když nezákonitě jednáte Když uposlechnete tyto nařízení vypomůžete nám velmi a zároveň tím získáte, že snadněji vyhrajeme stávku.

UMACA.

My możem wygrać jeśli się będziem unyj ściśle trzymać. Jeżeli będiem praw unyjnych słuchać i przestaniem szczepić ludni i krzywdzić własnoc budeky i zarosem trzymać w granicah praw tego kroju. Wszyscy będzie stroj kujacy musza udać sie do surych domów i starać sie być obecnijmi na unyjnych mityngoch dla dostania wszelkiech wiadomości

ZINE.

Mens iszgraisme, eugut mens Wisi laikiames pri Unios. Egut meus užlaikismia priaakimus Unios ne uzganti zmoniu ir ne dariti iszkados. ir usilaikismis welng zakona szito krazto Wisi zmonis asanto ant Straiko tegul aina namo ir tegul aina namo ir tegul ant mitingo, welng palespimo Wiresnibes del daxizmoimo wisokiu ziniu del wisu yera Egut mastas usilaikistia welng musu praszimia jus padestia izgraiti tan dldeli Sztraika Tamstos nnia negelbes jusu egut jus paktinittia i beda les savo sovalios.

Amalgamated Meat Gutters & Butcher Workmen of N. A.

New City Printing Office — 4559 Gross Avenue

Union notice to members asking them not to engage in violence.

strikebreakers. On July 25 the meatpacking union asked other unions to join in a sympathetic strike. The crafts, teamsters, and freight handlers all joined. The employers raised the pay rate for strikebreakers to five dollars a day. The rate before the strike had been $1.85 a day. The union opened relief stations with funds of 4700 dollars a week given by the Chicago Federation of Labor.

July 31 saw a hand to hand battle fought between 3000 strikers and 100 police. This started when union men saw two strikebreakers heading for home. The next day nonunion workers shot two strikers. In response nonunion workers were beaten through out the area. The Deering Street police station was attacked. At 47th and Loomis motormen refused to pick up strikebreakers and the crowds then attacked and beat the strikebreakers.

Teamsters refused to deliver ice to retail merchants who sold beef from the major meatpacking companies. Attacks were made on delivery wagons in the city. Retailers represented by Oscar Meyer and James Agar of the Meat Dealers Association went to the owners in an attempt to negotiate peace. The meatpacker owners replied they wished to reduce the average wage of skilled workers from $6.50 to $5.50 a day.

The strike now began to drag out with sporadic instances of violence. At the western entrance to the Stock Yards, 43rd and Paulina, 4000 men charged 150 police and battled for two hours. Three strikers were severely injured. Nonunion workers killed two strikers and seriously wounded two aboard a train heading for the Loop. At the end of August a nonunion worker was killed when he was thrown into the Chicago river.

On September 5 a settlement to end the strike was agreed to by the union and packers. Wages of skilled men were to remain the same and as many union workers as possible would be returned to their jobs. The companies would be allowed to pay the unskilled workers as they wished. This agreement was voted on September 6th and the union announced its overwhelming rejection. The union's executive board overruled this vote and ended the strike. Even after the formal end of the strike violence occurred. On September 12 a major riot took place when 1500 union members attacked a street car carrying blacks to the packing house. Many were severely hurt.

The union president, Michael Donnelly, criticized union members and leaders for the loss. This loss was a big blow to the new Amalgamated Meat Cutters Union. Efforts to organize workers in the pre-World War I years would suffer. There were positive

OPPOSITE PAGE

Strikers attack strikebreakers delivering meat.

effects. The strike generated interest in the industry and Upton Sinclair wrote a series of articles which detailed the disgusting conditions of the packing centers. These articles were published as *The Jungle* and gained wide readership that included President Roosevelt. The public reduced their consumption of meat and they placed political pressure to correct the sanitary conditions of the packing houses. This resulted in the nation's first pure food law, the Meat Inspection Act of 1906. Meat eaten by the public was cleaned up but this did little to help the conditions of meatpacking workers.

GARMENT WORKERS STRIKE (1910)

The years before World War I saw two important and violent strikes in Chicago's biggest industry - clothing manufacture. This industry employed 35,000 workers, mainly women. Most of the plants were small with 40 to 50 workers working under sweatshop conditions. The major employer was Hart, Schaffner & Marx which was the largest clothing manufacture in the United States. This company employed about 7500 workers and contracted work out to several dozen shops in the city. The management of these shops had the authority to change wages at will. On September 22, 1910, the pants-seamers at a Hart, Schaffner & Marx shop at 18th and Halsted received a penny a hour wage cut. All 17 women, mainly immigrant, walked out starting a battle which eventually involved 30,000 workers.

There was a great deal of discontent among the workforce due to low wages, long hours, and terrible working conditions. Many of the small garment shops had poor lighting, no ventilation, and filthy conditions. The United Garment Workers (UGW) had tried to organize many of the plants for several months but this union had many limitations to overcome. The UGW had been thoroughly defeated in an earlier strike in 1904-1905 which the teamsters had transformed to a general strike. Leadership of the UGW came from the native born skilled workers and had trouble organizing the unskilled immigrants from eastern Europe. The national union held off support of this new strike until they were forced to become involved.

The 1910 strike spread to shops around the city and support was forthcoming from many. Mayor Fred Busse and the City Council endorsed the union position and allowed city facilities to be used by the strikers. The Chicago Federation of Labor provided food and fuel for the union. Hull-House provided a daily meeting place for the strikers and city womens' groups held fund raising dances for the strike.

As the strike continued violence began. Strikers threw bricks into factories which were operating. The companies began to recruit out-of-state strikebreakers. These strikebreakers made their home inside the shops. Many of the nonstrikers who lived in Chicago were attacked by union members on their way home. The companies hired off-duty police and others to protect their workers while traveling from work. In

Union members picket clothing manufacture. The strikers were prohibited from picketing in much of the city.

December a private detective killed a striker who was insulting two workers going home. The funeral procession for the dead striker, Charles Lazinskas, drew 30,000 to the West Side. A week later another striker was killed by police when he attempted to enter the Kuppenheimer factory. A great deal of conflict arose over parading and picketing by the strikers. The strikers would picket and whistle past factories and the homes of nonstrikers. Police constantly made arrests and tried to limit these public displays. Charges of police brutality were made by the strikers and others working to aid the battle.

Hart, Schaffner & Marx attempted to start negotiations with the union which were mediated by the city council. In late December a teenager driving a wagon to a nonunion shop was shot to death. Two more died before the end of the strike. A bystander walking by some non-strikers was shot and a guard escorting some workers was killed. Finally a settlement with Hart, Schaffner & Marx was made on January 14, 1911. The agreement called for the reinstatement of all strikers and no discrimination against union members. Issues of wages and working conditions were to be given to an Arbitration Committee. This did not finally settle the entire strike because most of the clothing manufactures had not signed the agreement. In early February the leaders of the UGW called off the strike. Most of the 15,000 workers still on strike felt betrayed.

This strike had several ramifications. Some of the larger companies such as Hart, Schaffner & Marx realized unions in their plants could have benefits. When the strike was over Schaffner said:

The fundamental cause of the strike was that the workers had no satisfactory channel through which minor grievances, exactions and petty tyrannies of underbosses, could be taken up and amicably adjusted. [I] had been badly informed of conditions ... [and I] concluded the strike should have occurred much sooner.

This strike had made many leaders militant and radicalized. Many members of the UGW were dissatisfied with the conservative leadership of the national union. In 1914 this dissention came to a head at the union's convention in Nashville, Tennessee. Led by Chicago strike veterans, particularly Sidney Hillman, a majority of workers left the UGW and formed a new union, the Amalgamated Clothing Workers of America. This new union would become was of the nation's most important.

GARMENT WORKER STRIKE (1915)

In 1915, in addition to large manufacturers, the clothing industry employed about 25,000 workers in 400 small shops. The new Amalgamated Clothing Workers wanted to an agreement with the small shops which would be similar to the Hart agreement. The union called for: 1) a reduction of the work week to 48 hours from 52; 2) a 25

The Streets of Chicago

percent wage increase; 3) distribution of work over slack seasons; and 4) recognition of the union. The employers refused to arbitrate. The union called a strike on September 28. The United Garment Workers opposed the strike but the Amalgamated had the majority of members. The police and companies were more aggressive than in 1910. The police used horses and motorcycles to charge crowds which gathered on street corners. To keep out strikers the shops locked their doors creating fire hazards.

Police and strikers fought street battles everyday. On October 2 a crowd of 1000 attempted to enter the Loop over the Adams Street bridge and were driven back by police. The strikers threw carbolic acid balls at police and nonstrikers. On October 26 shortly after four nonstrikers were beaten a striker was shot to death by nonunion workers. During the first 30 days of the strike police reports showed 339 assaults, 1023 complaints, and 876 arrests. Over 1100 had been arrested by the middle of November. Daily newspapers would report the toll of strikers, nonstrikers and police that had been injured. A full list published at the beginning of November had 493 names and their injuries. Other strikes had been worse for mass violence but this strike involved large scale individual violence spread out over a wide area. The City Council began a hearing which the police chief denounced as bias. Chief Schuettler released a statement which said:

The hearings of the council committee have been so one sided that the strikers believe they have everything their own way. No wonder the strikers and strikebreakers think they can go the limit. There has been more violence since the hearing began that has marked any strike for years. The council committee will hear only the cases of girls beaten by the police, but they haven't been interested in the 500 cases of assaults by strikers.

Sidney Hillman, worried that he was losing public support for the strike released a call to the strikers which said:

Violence must stop. You have the right to picket peacefully but I urge you not to congregate in great numbers around the strike bound plants or conduct yourselves in a manner that might be provocative of violence. In the interest of the cause nearest of our hearts violence must stop. Our cause is so just that we are bound to win. Justice ultimately must prevail.

A second death in the strike occurred when strikers killed a union member by mistake. Michael Guszkowski, a young union tailor, was dragged from a saloon by eight men who kicked and clubbed him to death. Ten union members were indicted for the crime.

The strike came to a close in mid-December when many of the clothing companies agreed to demands with the exception of union recognition. A 48 hour week was agreed on and grievances were to be handled by a shop committee. The eleven week strike had resulted in 2 deaths, several hundred injured, and thousands of dollars of property destroyed. The Amalgamated Clothing Workers had not been successful in union recognition but had gained valuable experience for the future.

HENRICI STRIKES (1914)

The Henrici strikes were a series of strikes involving Loop restaurants. The basic issue of the strikes were recognition of the Restaurant Waitresses Union along with higher pay. The strikes were violent and clarified Illinois law concerning boycotts.

The first walkout took place February 5, 1914 at Henrici's restaurant located at 71 W. Randolph. Immediate arrests took place when the waitresses attempted to picket outside the restaurant. The union charged the police with brutality. Some of the waitresses suffered broken legs and arms when they were arrested. One day the police dragged the women a half block and pulled their arms from the sockets. The arrests briefly stopped when they started to picket with flags. Women from the Hull-House settlement began to help out on the picket lines. Other unions involving bakers, waiters, and cooks walked out in support.

The union decided to expand the strike to the 35 restaurants that were members of the Restaurant Keepers Association. The goal would be union recognition and better pay. The union was opposed to tips. The union charged that in some of the restaurants women were forced to wear high necked skirts with tight collars. This type of dress would not allow the waitresses anyplace to put coins. The owners would keep the tips.

One plan advanced by the union was to circulate 'dry' petitions since all the restaurants served liquor and most were allied with breweries. Hull-House requested the use of policewomen when dealing with the pickets. The Womens City Club agreed to investigate the brutality charges and the use of force. Policewomen were assigned to the pickets on February 27 and they continued the pattern of arrests. Another union tactic was to pressure the city's health department to enforce health codes against basement bakeries.

As March began 11 unions agreed to support the waitresses. These included the drivers of delivery wagons for grocers, dairies, butchers, and brewers. Building engineers in the buildings where restaurants were located also threw in their support. There was 150 arrests by this time.

The waitresses asked a for a boycott of the restaurants by other unions as well as customers. On April 6 judges ruled picking which drew crowds was illegal. It was legal to print flyers calling attention to the labor dispute. The waitresses could not picket on Randolph Street. The decision barred the union pickets from talking so they

The Chicago Daily Tribune

THE WORLD'S GREATEST NEWSPAPER

FRIDAY, FEBRUARY 6, 1914.

Union Girls Picket Boycotted Loop Restaurant.

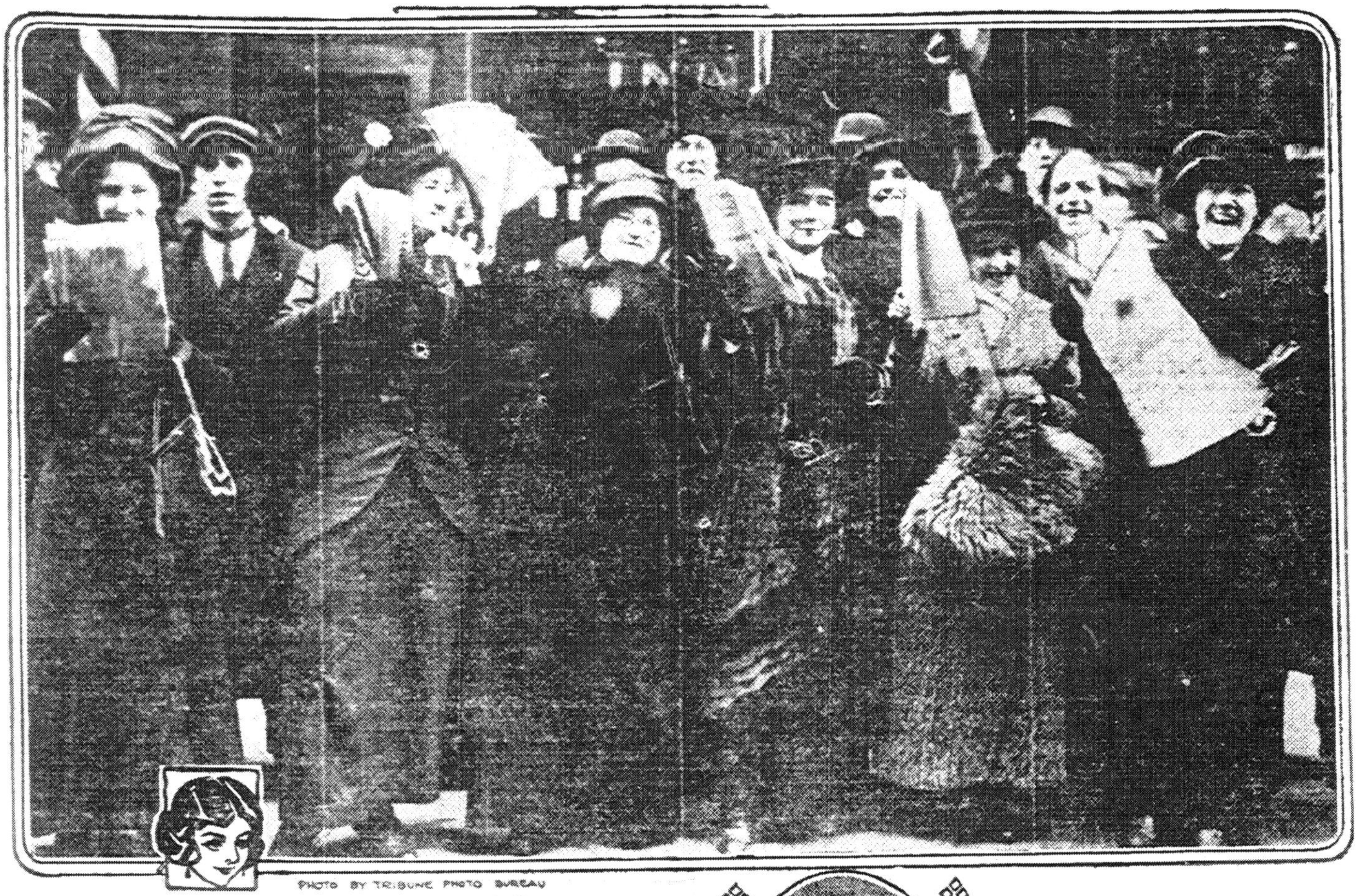

PHOTO BY TRIBUNE PHOTO BUREAU

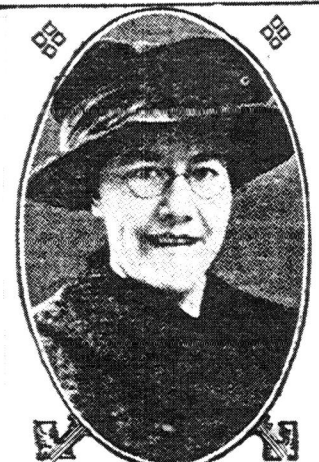

CARRIE ALEXANDER
PRESIDENT WAITRESSES' LOCAL

Newspaper photo of the Henrici Restaurant strike (1914) which clarified Illinois law concerning labor boycotts.

STRIKE ON AT HENRICI'S.

Don't Eat Under Police **!** Protection

We want $8 for six days' work. The order of Judges McGoorty, Windes, and Baldwin PERMITS the waitresses to print these words.

WE CAN'T SPEAK THEM
? ? ? ? ? WHAT OF IT ? ? ? ? ?

Henrici strikers were arrested for handing out this handbill at elevated train platforms (1914).

The Streets of Chicago

handed out handbills like the one reprinted on page 80. The police continued to arrest those handing out flyers. Four waitresses were charged with conspiracy when they wore yellow raincoats with large letters on the back that said:

ON STRIKE AT HENRICI'S
HENRICI PAY $7 FOR 7 DAYS
WE WANT $8 FOR 6 DAYS

The courts enjoined silent picketing on May 9. A general boycott by all unions in the city concerned with deliveries was called. This involved the teamsters, laundry drivers, chauffeurs, and others. After a few days most restaurants agreed to some wage hikes, a day off, and improvements in working conditions. The Waitress union was not recognized however. The Henrici strikes were important as it clarified the Illinois law on boycotts and free speech as it relates to labor disputes. It also proved to be a powerful strike by a womens' trade union which was backed up by unions which had primarily male members.

BATTLE

TO ORGANIZE

INDUSTRY

4

RACE AND LABOR WAR IN CHICAGO (1919)

World War I ended on November 11, 1918. Soon afterwards legions of soldiers headed back to their hometowns. This mass of men coming on the labor market coupled with cutbacks in factory production caused an increase of competition for jobs. In Chicago this tension took on racial overtones. The black neighborhood in Chicago was called Bronzeville and contained 100,000 residents. The area was located from 21st to 63rd streets and Washington Park to Wentworth. Wentworth Avenue was the racial dividing line with whites living to the east. Carl Sandburg, a reporter for the *Daily News*, wrote a series of articles about Bronzeville in late July, 1919, warning that a racial explosion was near.

July had already been violent month in the Chicago area. A strike that began on July 8 at Argo Corn Products located in a suburb just outside Chicago left three dead. The mayor of Argo was forced to flee the town by the outraged wives of strikers. The Chicago Stock Yards were hit by a walkout of 10,000 in the middle of the month over the issue of police presence in the plants. Another 10,000 walked out at International Harvester. Crane company saw 6500 strike at three plants. Five were killed at the Standard Steel strike that month in the Chicago border city of Hammond, Indiana. The weather on July 27, was 98 degrees and thousands of Chicagoans were at the beach. The 29th Street beach was one of many along Chicago's lakefront and has an informal dividing line for black and white bathers. A black boy swam into the white area and was killed by a stone thrown by a white youth. This set off five days and nights of intense racial fighting. Warring gangs surged back and forth Wentworth Avenue raining violence onto the opposing neighborhood. The first day of rioting saw two dead and 50 hurt. Both black and white former soldiers used their war skills fighting each other. On the South Side telegraph wires were cut. Elevated trains and street cars ceased to run.

The map on page 84 shows the area of fighting which ranged over most of the South Side. Two days after the first stone was thrown 11 whites were dead, 15 blacks, and 300 injured. On the third day Mayor Thompson sent militia companies to the area.

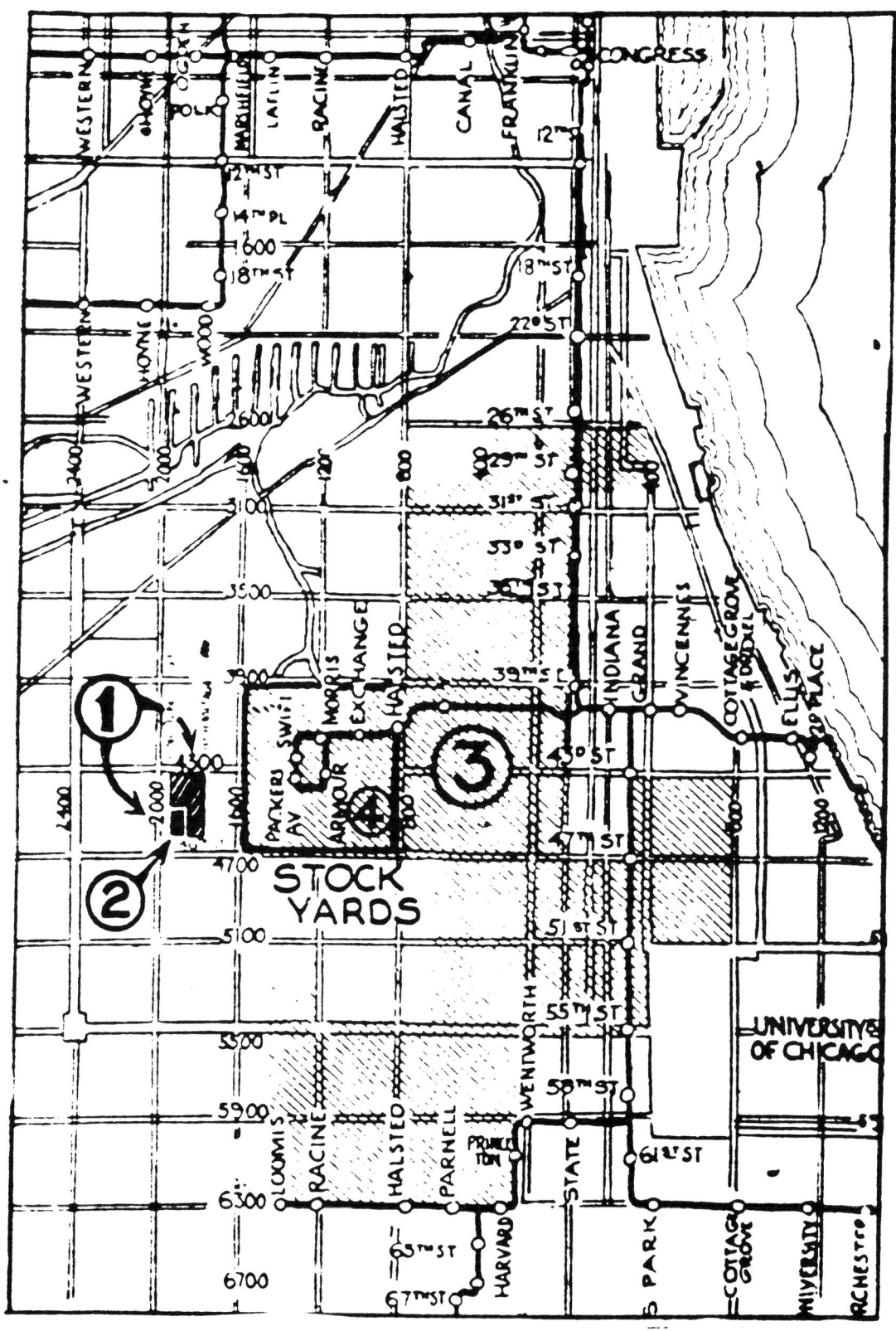

1919 Race Riot

1. The fire zone boundaries. 2. It was the worst on Honore Street between 45th and 46th streets. 3. This is the riot area patrolled by militia. 4. Location of Stock Yards.

Over 1000 were left homeless in the rioting and arson (1919).

One white man who did not move fast enough was cut to pieces by bayonets. On August 2, black gangs surged into the Polish and Lithuanian neighborhoods in the Back-of-the-Yards. In the area of 46th and Hermitage 49 homes were torched and burned. This attack left 948 people homeless. The IWW also was blamed for this arson. The Poles and Lithuanians had broken the strike in July against the meatpackers when they accepted the agreement. Some felt the IWW were getting revenge against a neighborhood of "strikebreakers." After the arson the meatpackers temporarily banned blacks from working in the Yards in an attempt to stop the bloodshed.

At the end of the racial battles 14 whites and 22 blacks had been killed. Most had been shot or beaten to death by the opposing race while the militia killed the remainder. The known injured were 537 and over 1000 were homeless. Following the riots the Chicago Federation of Labor issued a proclamation:

The profiteering meat packers of Chicago are responsible for the race riots which have disgraced our city. It is the outcome of their deliberate attempt to disrupt the union labor movement in the yards.
Organized labor has no quarrel with the colored worker. The only way for the packers to end the race riots is to maintain a closed shop. They must get negroes into the union and pay them union scale. If this is not done, there will be more race riots.

World War I brought wartime prosperity to the steel industry and the mills were working at capacity. With the exception of a few crafts the steel industry was largely unorganized. The AFL decided to have an organizing drive and formed a committee of 24 unions, all of which claimed jurisdiction in the industry. The committee, the National Committee for Organizing the Iron and Steel Workers (NCOISW), was headed by John Fitzpatrick, President of the CFL. Secretary of the committee was a radical unionist, William Z. Foster, who later became chairman of the Communist Party USA. The NCOISW began passing out membership cards in the steel districts including Chicago in late 1918. Six months after the formation of the NCOISW almost 100,000 had signed up.

In early August, 1919, the NCOISW formulated a list of demands to be presented to the industry. They are shown on page 87. The NCOISW attempted to meet with Elbert Gary, Chairman of United States Steel, but he refused to see the union organizers. Gary said he wanted an open shop and would never negotiate with the union. The AFL committee called for a strike beginning September 21, 1919. At the end of September between 300,000 and 350,000 workers had walked out from a total of 500,000 in the industry. The strike included 75,000 in the Chicago area. The mills in Gary, Indiana were reduced to 50 percent capacity by October 1. Large numbers of blacks were imported to work the mills from the Deep South and from the black neighborhoods of Chicago. Most of the AFL unions did not admit blacks. By

OLVASSA! ČITAJTE! LEGGETE! CITESTE! CZITAJ!

IRON AND STEEL WORKERS
BULLETIN No. 2

Published by National Committee for Organizing Iron and Steel Workers

JOHN FITZPATRICK, Chairman
Chicago, Ill.

PITTSBURGH, PA., JULY 30, 1919

WILLIAM Z. FOSTER, Secretary-Treasurer
303 Magee Bldg., Pittsburgh, Pa.

IMPORTANT! ATTENTION!

The following propositions, adopted by the National Committee for Organizing Iron and Steel Workers, at the meeting in Pittsburgh, July 20th, 1919, will be presented to the big steel corporations as soon as conferences can be arranged between them and the unions. These propositions are general in character and are subject to development when the various organizations prepare their respective trade demands.

1. Right of Collective Bargaining.
2. Reinstatement of All Men Discharged for Union Activities, with Pay for Time Lost.
3. The Eight Hour Day.
4. One Day's Rest in Seven.
5. Abolition of 24-Hour Shifts.
6. Increases in Wages Sufficient to Guarantee American Standards of Living.
7. Standard Scales of Wages for All Crafts and Classifications of Workers.
8. Double Rates of Pay for All Overtime Work and for Work on Sundays and Holidays.
9. Check-off System of Collecting Union Dues and Assessments.
10. Principles of Seniority to Apply in Maintaining, Reducing and Increasing Working Forces.
11. Abolition of Company Unions.
12. Abolition of Physical Examination of Applicants for Employment.

When in force, these reforms will make the steel industry one of the best in the country to work in. To achieve them will require the co-operation of every iron and steel worker. Be a man and do your part. Join the American Federation of Labor at once, and get all your fellow workers to do likewise.

LAVORATORI DI FERRO E ACCIAIO

Le seguenti proposte, adottate dal Comitato Nazionale, per la organizzazione dei lavoratori di ferro ed acciaio, alla riunione di Pittsburgh, 20 Luglio 1919, sara' presentata alle grandi Compagnie di acciaio. Queste proposte sono generali in carattere, e sono soggette a sviluppo quando le varie organizzazioni preparano le loro rispettive domande commerciali.

1—Diritto di collettivo contratto.
2—Riammissione di tutti gli operai licenziati per attivita' all'unione, con paga per il tempo perduto.
3—Otto ore al giorno di lavoro.
4—Un giorno di riposo ogni sette.
5—Abolizione di ventiquattr'ore di cambio.
6—Aumento di paga sufficiente a garantire il tenore di vita americana.
7—Scala progressiva di Paga per ogni specie e classificazione di lavoratori.
8—Doppia rata di paga per l'extra lavoro e per il lavoro della Domenica o Giorni festivi.
9—Sistema di marcare la collettazione di tasse o altri pesi.
10—Principio dell'anzianita' nell'applicazione di mantenere, ridurre o aumentare la paga degli operai.
11—Abolizione delle Unioni della Compagnia.
12—Abolizione dell'esame fisico per coloro che domandano impiego.

Quando queste riforme saranno applicate l'industria dell'acciaio diverra' una delle migliori del nostro Paese. Per raggiungere questi scopi e' necessaria la cooperazione di ciascun lavoratore in ferro e acciaio. Siate un uomo e fate la vostra parte. Unitevi alla Federazione Americana del Lavoro, subito, e consigliate i vostri amici lavoratori di far come voi.

ŽELEZNÝ A OCEĽOVÝ ROBOTNÍCI.

Na 20-ho Júla t. r. v Pittsburgh-u vydržiavanej schôdzi prijal Medzinárodný Výbor pre železných a oceľových robotnikov nasledovný návrh a predloží veľkým oceľovým spoločnostiam. Tento návrh je všeobecný v jeho povahe a je predmet, keď všelijaké organizácie sa prichystajú na dotyčne požadované pochody.

1) Správne požadovanie svojich práv.
2) Nazpät prijatia do Unionského účinkovania prepustených, s platom za ztratený čas.
3) Osemhodinový pracovný čas.
4) Každých sedem dní, jeden deň na odpočinutie.
5) Vyzdvihnutie 24-hodinového presťahovania.
6) Podvýška pláce, k zabezpečeniu poriadnemu americkému životbytiu.
7) Pomerená pláca pre každého remeselného a triedneho robotníka.
8) Duplovaná pláca prez čas, v nedeľu alebo vo sviatok.
9) Ček od každých Unionských príspevkov alebo daní prijatých.
10) Základ zadržania starších robotníkov, sníženia alebo podvihnutia robotnej sily.
11) Vyzdvihnutie Kompanickej Union-i.
12) Vyzdvihnutie lekárskeho prepatrenia, hlásiacich sa o robotu.

Jestli tieto podmienky budú ustanovené, oceľové ústavy budú v celej krajine najlepšie v nich robiť. Ale k tomu vyhoveniu požaduje každého železo a oceľového robotníka spolupôsobiť. Buďte teda mužom a čiňte vašu čiastku. Vstúpte do Amerického Robotníckeho Spolku doraz, a nahovárajte aj vašich spolubratov, aby tiež pristúpili.

Steel worker organizing flyer listing demands (1919).

EXTRA EXTRA	EXTRA EXTRA
G R A N D I O S O M I T I N Literario Musical EL DOMINGO 13 de DICIEMBRE Alas 3 DE LA TARDE CROATIAN HALL 96th Street & COMMERCIAL AVENUE La seccion mexicana del Steel Workers Organizing Committee ha organizado este atractivo programa patrocinado por el Honorable Consul de Mexico en Chicago y en el que tomaran parte importantes oradores de la union y notables artistas mexicanos. Es de vital importancia que todos los trabajadores mexicanos y sus familias asistan a esta funcion en que quedaran enterados de la enorme transcendencia de la campana de organizacion industrial que se esta llevando a cabo. CERCIORESE Y DIVIERTASE ENTERAMENTE GRATIS La orquestra ' Los Cubanos ' deleitara al publico con su popular musica mexicana. 1. El Honorable consul de Mexico Sr. Antonio L. Schmidt tendra a su cargo importante discurso sobre " La posicion actual del mexicano en los E.U. 2. Pieza de musica. 3. El abogado Hurscovicks hablara en espanol de la union. 4. Pieza de musica. 5. Canciones por las hermanas Avila. 6. Breves palabras por George Patterson. Pte. De la union. 7. Pieza de musica. 8. Monologo dramatico, por el actor Jose Nieto. 9. Discurso, Charles Kyser, Representante del Steel Workers Committee. 10. Pieza de musica. 11. Jugete comico, por el actor Jose Nieto. 12. Pieza de musica. 13. Jarabe tapatio por una pareja de ninos. 14. Canciones. Hnas. Avila. 15. Pieza de musica. Debido a la seriedad del acto se ruega al publico guardar el mayor silencio posible ENTRADA GRATIS NO HABRA COLECTA ENTRADA GRATIS	Big Meeting Musical Literary Sunday December 13 At 3 in the afternoon Croatian Hall 96th Street & Commercial Avenue The Mexican session of steel workers organizing committee has organized this attractive program funded by the honorable Mexican consul in Chicago in which there will be Mexican actors and important union members. It is of vital importance that all Mexican workers and their families attend this event in which they're going to be informed of the enormous transaction of the industrial organizing company that is taking place now. GET INFORMED ENTIRELY FREE The orchestra ' Los Cubanos'(The Cubans) will play for the public with their popular Mexican music. 1. The Honorable Mexican Consul Mr. Antonio L. Schmidt will have an important speech relating on ' The actual position of the Mexicans in the United States. 2. Piece of song 3. Attorney Hurscovicks will speak about the Union in spanish. 4. Piece of song 5. Songs by the Avila sisters. 6. A few words by George Patterson. Pertaining to the union. 7. Piece of Song 8. Dramatic act , by actor Jose Nieto. 9. Speech, Charles Kyser, representative of the Steel Workers Committee. 10. Piece of song. 11. Comical play, by actor Jose Nieto. 12. Piece of song. 13. Mexican cultural dance (jarabe tapatio) by a couple of kids. 14. Songs, by the Avila sisters. 15. Piece of song. According to the seriousness of the act we urge the public to keep the noise down. FREE ENTRANCE NO COLLECTIONS FREE ENTRANCE

Bilingual flyer asking steelworkers to come to a rally in South Chicago (from CFL).

late October 75 percent of the work was being done by blacks and 95 percent of them had not worked in the mills prior to the strike.

During this time radical politics became mixed in with the strike. William Z. Foster of NCOISW was a known radical and the companies attacked his connection to the union. The United States had intervened in the Soviet Union civil war at this time so the issue of Bolsheviks and radicals was on the public's mind. On October 14, a large crowd of World War I veterans attacked the IWW headquarters at 8749 Commercial. This office was near the U.S.Steel mill in South Chicago. They destroyed it. President Wilson sent federal troops into Gary and they stayed in the city until the end of the strike. A total of 18 workers were killed in Gary during the course of strike.

Resources of U.S.Steel combined with the government's military support overwhelmed the strikers by the end of the year. A majority of strikers had gone back to work by January and the strike was officially called off on January 8, 1920. This strike was a failure for several reasons. The exclusion of blacks from AFL unions made it easy for blacks to be recruited as strikebreakers. Trying to organize the industry based on two dozen different craft unions was also a mistake. Workers in mass production industries such as steel, auto, and rubber would have to be organized in one industry wide union.

The U.S. Senate investigated the 1919 steel strike. The Senate concluded the wages were sufficient but the hours were too long. The Senate report stated the workers had a right to have their own representatives to present grievances. Radicals were accused of being behind the strike. The Senate recommended: 1) aid to workers to buy homes; 2) an Americanization law to require education of foreign and native illiterates; 3) require the deporting of aliens who do not learn English in five years; 4) set up a agency similar to the war labor board; and 5) pass an anti-revolution law.

MEATPACKING STRIKE OF 1921

After the 1904 meatpacking strike described in Chapter 3 the working conditions and pay remained stagnant until World War I. During the War most of the workers became members of the Amalgamated Meat Cutters (AMC) and wage gains were made. Stock Yard workers were also helped by the wartime labor board which President Wilson had set up for the meatpacking industry. This board was intended to prevent any strikes during the war. During the course of the war the board granted a eight-hour day and a 40 hour week. With the general wage increase achieved during the war and with overtime the packing house workers saw a 50 percent gain in their income by 1921.

As 1921 began the Stock Yard Big Four -- Armour, Swift, Morris, and Wilson, told the government labor board that wartime wage agreements would be void at the end of the year. Legal authority for the board expired on September 1. The packing houses complained they were losing millions and wages had to be reduced. In response the

The Streets of Chicago

AMC announced a strike to begin November 15, 1921. Further wage cuts came and were endorsed by the company shop councils which had been installed to resolve grievances. Armour had started this shop representation plan and other packers had copied it. These plans had plant conference boards to compete with the union. These boards were made up of equal number of employer and employee representatives. From the plant boards, members of the general assembly were chosen. This assembly had endorsed the a 10 percent wage cut. The union finally walked out at the beginning of December. The AMC claimed 12,000 had walked out. The companies claimed a tenth of that figure had joined the dispute.

The Stockyard area immediately became a battleground. Near Davis Square (44th and Ashland) strikers and police charged each other fighting with clubs, night sticks, and stones. Police shot mainly over heads but still two were wounded. An elevated train bringing strikebreakers to the Yards was attacked with stones and bricks by strikers at 40th and Wallace. At the end of the day a both sides had a total of nine shot and 27 were hurt.

The next day was even more violent. Police on horses and motorcycles charged into crowds who had gathered at the 43rd and Ashland corner exit to the stockyards. Police were stoned from upper story windows and women with large sacks of red pepper threw it on officers to blind them. Strikers broke picket fences apart and used them as clubs to knock police from their motorcycles. Four snipers shot at police from adjoining houses. One striker was shot by police and taken into custody. Battle raged between the sides for over a hour. The crowd screamed, "The cossacks! Damn them! Kill them!". Non-strikers found their homes surrounded by crowds and had their windows broken. Police fired 300 shots into the air and made hundreds of arrests. At the end of the day 150 had been injured. Police said the only reason there had not been more violence was because it was payday at the stockyards. Workers not honoring the strike appeared in ones and twos to pick up their checks instead of appearing in mass at the beginning of the day.

The packers were importing thousands of strikebreakers, mainly black. The AMC had generally excluded blacks from the union so it was easy for the packers to bring in strikebreakers from the Black Belt. Racial division in the stockyards was extreme. Early in the strike a group of strikers took a black strikebreaker and threw him into Bubbly Creek. This 'creek' led into the Chicago River and was a depository of the fifth and residue of the packers. The strikers threw stones and killed their victim. After two days of violence the energy of the strike was nearly spent. By the end of the year the strike was over as workers drifted back to work. Many of the strikers found their jobs permanently replaced by those recruited to break the strike. This strike failure ended union representation in the stockyards until the late 1930s when the CIO sponsored the Packinghouse Workers Organizing Committee.

OPPOSITE PAGE Police battle strikers in the Stockyards (1921).

MOB INFLUENCE IN THE UNIONS (1930s)

During the decade of the 1920s labor battles were rare. The end of the war slowed industrial demand decline. This situation was made worse as servicemen returned to the homefront. This turned the labor shortage which had helped unions to a labor surplus. Unions were also troubled by the scare of the socialism of the new Soviet Union. People who spoke up for the union risked being accused of being a radical. Established unions started to settle into American life and provide service beyond the workplace. In 1922 the Amalgamated Clothing Workers started the Amalgamated Trust and Savings Bank in Chicago. This was the first bank started by a union organization. The bank provided mortgage money for many workers as well as union halls. In July, 1926, the CFL started the "Voice of Labor", radio station WCFL which was the first such station in the country. Chicagoans could hear programs presented by local unions as well as popular entertainment.

The reputations of unions suffered in the post-War era due in part to corrupt union leaders and labor racketeering. Media and government reports attempted to convince workers that collective bargaining was a sham to get union dues. In Chicago union bosses and employers were accused of collusion and extortion in the building trades and service industries. The crime syndicate made moves to control several Chicago unions, killing those who stood in the way.

Two Chicago unions who suffered this fate included: Local 569 of the Hoisting and Portable Engineers; and the Scrap Iron and Junk Handlers'. The Hoisting and Portable Engineers was a key union for organized crime to control. Members of the union operated the large cranes on construction projects. Construction companies, operating on deadlines, would be subject to extortion if the syndicate could control the key machinery on the site.

Dennis Bruce Zeigler was the leader of Local 569 and was considered honest and no friend of the mob. Starting in 1930 Zeigler began receiving death threats when he refused to take bribes. William E. Maloney, who later became leader of the International Union of Operating Engineers, wanted Local 569 under his domain. Zeigler rejected these demands. An increase in death threats caused the police to put a guard at Zeigler's house for 18 months. The police guard was suddenly withdrawn in February, 1933. On February 24, Zeigler, who lived at 3634 N. Tripp Avenue, was walking to his house after getting off the streetcar. Streetlights were mysteriously off on North Tripp that night. A witness saw a figure jump from a car and fire three shots into Zeigler, killing him. This crime was never solved and the union soon was lost to the mob.

The Scrap Iron and Junk Handlers' union was another target for mob control. This union was useful for the syndicate as a means for both extortion from business which needed their services as well as a conduit for the disposal of stolen property.

2 CENTS PAY NO MORE!

Chicago Daily Tribune
THE WORLD'S GREATEST NEWSPAPER

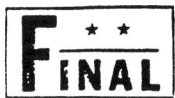
FINAL

VOLUME XCVIII—NO. 294 C — SATURDAY, DECEMBER 9, 1939.—28 PAGES — PRICE TWO CENTS

ATTORNEY SHOT; UNION ROW

Repel Offensive on Karelian Isthmus

Union Ex-Leader Shot
(Story on page 1.)

Leon R. Cooke (left), lawyer and former secretary of Scrap Iron and Junk Handlers' union, who was shot while in union offices, and Jack Rubinstein present secretary who was seized for questioning.

NEWS SUMMARY of The Tribune

LOCAL.
- Union's affairs probed after shooting of lawyer. Page 1.
- Election board tells how plan to save $100,000 on printing bill went awry. Page 3.
- Brooks to make race for senate on Republican ticket. Page 2.
- Judges Holland and McGarry spend day in empty courtrooms. Page 4.
- Ten thousand Chicago school children see stock show wonders. Page 11.
- Federal trust buster moves to launch Chicago building inquiry in January. Page 12.
- City engineers propose new super-highway plan for south side. Page 29.
- Deaths and obituaries. Page 26.

WAR SITUATION.
- Finns halt Reds on Karelian isthmus; admit losses on two other fronts. Page 1.
- Fourteen ship losses disclosed; German U-boat damages new British destroyer. Page 1.
- Scandinavian ships retreat from Finnish waters to beat soviet blockade. Page 2.
- League opens trial today of Russia, charged with aggression against Finland. Page 2.

DOMESTIC.
- Ohio governor assails Roosevelt in clash over relief. Page 1.
- David Lawrence, Democratic boss in Pennsylvania, found not guilty of graft and blackmail. Page 2.

WASHINGTON.
- Immediate quiz demanded on New Orleans WPA graft. Page 2.
- Secretary Hull protests to Britain on naval blockade. Page 8.
- Naval shakeup will make Admiral James O. Richardson commander of United States fleet. Page 8.

SPORTS.
- White Sox get Solters; Al Todd is traded to Cubs. Page 17.
- Thirty grim New York Giants reach Milwaukee for battle. Page 17.
- Chicago or Northwestern to be host at Big Ten outdoor track. Page 17.
- Day evens account with Angott in return bout. Page 17.
- Oak Park five loses; Proviso, Morton triumph. Page 18.
- Bruins' goals in last period defeat Red Wings, 3-0. Page 18.
- Petsy Clark, Jim Phelan mentioned for Cardinal coaching job. Page 19.

EDITORIALS
Another Touch Succeeds; This is the Red McGee...

ADMIT GIVING GROUND ON TWO OTHER FRONTS

Claim 100 Russian Tanks Disabled.

WITH THE FINNISH ARMY ON THE KARELIAN FRONT, Dec. 8 (AP).—Stubbornly resisting Finns halted 700,000 Russians and disabled 100 Red tanks hurled at their Karelian isthmus defenses, but gave ground on two other fronts during the day, Finnish commanders reported tonight.

Red army troops trying to reach the Mannerheim line, a water defense system across the Karelian isthmus, were turned back with especially heavy fighting on the eastern sector along the Taipale river, an army communique said.

In the Gulf of Finland the Finns said the Russians occupied Suursaari (Hogland) Island after seven days of shelling and bombing.

[A Moscow communique said the Russians occupied the island four days ago.]

Villages on the island were said to have been leveled by the soviet big guns and air bombs. The island's defenders, however, made their escape, the communique said.

On the central front the Finns announced that Finnish forces were forced to withdraw from Suomussalmi, a village about 15 miles from the frontier.

Elsewhere, the communique said, there was no activity worth mentioning.

Heavy Artillery Roars.

Heavy artillery thundered on both sides of the front at Summa, a village 20 miles from the ancient Finnish city of Viipuri (Vyborg) and 40 miles within Finland.

Col. Alexander Mellbloom, commandant of the Viipuri sector, said the Russian advance had been halted momentarily, but expressed belief that Russia was bringing up fresh troops for a new assault.

OUR FAVORITE INDIAN

"KEEP IT UP, BIG CHIEF! I'M ALL FOR YOU! YIPPEE!"

'BOMB' TOSSED FROM WINDOW OF TRAIN AT BRIDGE ACROSS FIRTH

LONDON, Dec. 8 (AP).—Scottish police and military authorities tonight disclosed an apparent attempt to...

Tell How Plan to Cut Election Cost Is Balked

TESTIFIES DUES PAID BY REDS IN AMERICA ARE SENT TO RUSSIA

San Francisco, Cal., Dec. 8 (AP).—Miles G. Humphries, former communist and ousted union organizer...

Boss Hunted as Assailant; Dues Probed

(Pictures on page 2 and back page.)

Business affairs of the Scrap Iron and Junk Handlers' union were under official scrutiny last night after Attorney Leon R. Cooke, 27 years old, was shot and seriously wounded in the union headquarters at 3159 Roosevelt road.

At the Mount Sinai hospital Cooke said his assailant was John Martin, the union president. Martin fled after the shooting, and a search was started for him. Police said they believed he was accompanied by his stenographer, Mrs. Gladys Walsh, 609 Walnut street, Hinsdale, who was said to have witnessed the shooting. Martin is 45 years old and lives at 4620 South Wolcott avenue. He has been a clerk in the employ of the sanitary district for 22 years.

Indicted With Druggan.

Last August he was indicted with Terry Druggan and two others for conspiracy to conceal from revenue officers the fact that Druggan, a notorious bootlegger, was part owner of the Gambrinus brewery. The case is to be tried in February.

Cooke, whose home is at 1135 South Sacramento boulevard, was one of the organizers two years ago of the junk handlers' union, which is affiliated with the American Federation of Labor. He was secretary and treasurer last year but now holds no office in the union.

"I want to see Martin to protest his conduct of the union," Cooke said in the hospital. "I told him he ought to have obtained a pay raise for the men in one junkyard. He was stormy and in a little while we were scuffling. When he grabbed a gun I told him he was crazy and started to leave..."

Newspaper showing the arrest of Jack Ruby in connection with union killing.

Attorney Leon R. Cooke, an idealistic attorney, had organized the union in 1937 and had served as it's secretary. Jack Rubinstein was the present secretary and an agent of organized crime. Cooke went to the union headquarters at 3159 Roosevelt Road on December 8, 1939. He was angry at a sellout of workers the union had agreed to at one junkyard. Shots were fired and Cooke was mortally wounded, dying days later. Rubinstein was seized by police but charges were not filed. After the killing, with Rubinstein's help, Paul 'Red' Dorfman became President of the Scrap Handlers'. Dorfman, a former prizefighter, was the gambling boss of the North Side. He was a close associate of Tony Accardo and other mob figures. The Scrap Handlers' Union became part of the Teamsters soon after Dorfman took over. For the next ten years Jack Rubinstein did work for the mob in Chicago and then he moved to Dallas, Texas. He changed his name to Jack Ruby, and began to manage mob activities in Dallas.

In 1949 Jimmy Hoffa was president of the Michigan Teamsters and wanted national control of the union. He needed mob help to do it. According to the FBI, Paul Dorfman introduced Hoffa to mob figures in return for giving teamster insurance business to his son Allen. An insurance company, Union Casualty Company was set up in 1948 with Allen Dorfman in control. In 1949 Chicago Teamster Local 743 was the first contract signed by Dorfman's company to process claims for the Teamster's health, welfare, and pension funds. Hoffa threw Dorfman the business of the entire Central States Teamsters Fund a year later. Dorfman controlled loans from the funds. Under his guidance these teamster funds made hundreds of millions of dollars in loans for speculative real estate, friends of Teamster officials and Los Vegas casinos. Within a few years Allen Dorfman was a millionaire.

Rubinstein, now Jack Ruby, was working for Carlos Marcello, the Mob Boss of the southern states, in 1963. Attorney General Robert Kennedy had been attempting to get Marcello deported to Guatemala. He had been deported once before which almost resulted in his death, but he managed to escape back to the United States. His trial was to begin November 22, 1963, the same day as President Kennedy was to visit Dallas. Marcello and Hoffa had business dealings in the southern states. Hoffa also knew Ruby. His son, James P. Hoffa testified that, "I think my dad knew Jack Ruby ... so what?" In the days before November 22, Ruby made telephone calls to high ranking Teamster officials. The facts demonstrate the ties and connections between Ruby, Hoffa, and Marcello. When Lee Harvey Oswald was accused of assassinating President Kennedy on November 22, Jack Ruby killed Oswald. After Ruby silenced Oswald, Marcello continued to help Hoffa with legal troubles.

On January 20, 1983 it had been just over 43 years since Jack Rubinstein helped Paul Dorfman gain control of local union which would ally itself with the Teamster's Union. On that day, Allen Dorfman was shot to death in the parking lot of the Hyatt in Lincolnwood, just outside Chicago. He had recently been convicted of conspiracy to bride Senator Howard Cannon and of defrauding the Central States Teamster's Pension Fund. This was Chicago's 1081st gangland killing. It ended a story that began in 1939 with Jack Ruby's involvement in the killing for which resulted in mob control of the Scrap Handlers' union.

THE MEMORIAL DAY MASSACRE OF 1937

In 1934 the Blue Eagle Lodge of the Amalgamated Association of Iron, Steel and Tin Workers (AAISTW) was the first and only local union in any of the South Chicago steel mills. This local union was located on Chicago's South side at the Republic Steel plant employed 1700 employees. The Depression had hit Chicago and the steel industry was largely unorganized. The only union was the AAISTW which was old, weak, and unrecognized by the steel companies.

In July, 1936, the Steel Workers Organizing Committee (SWOC) was established by John L. Lewis, leader of the CIO. Lewis, President of the Coal Miners' Union, had recruited 150 organizers and the miners' union contributed $500,000 for the organizing drive. The steel industry had many 'Employee Representation Plans' which were in effect company unions. The steel industry resisted the new SWOC union drive bitterly. Republic Steel declared war on the organizing drive (see Appendix B-5 for the Republic Steel letter to employees concerning SWOC). Across the country the company unions collapsed as workers signed up to join the SWOC. At the Republic plant in Chicago the SWOC local was chartered as Local 1033. (The SWOC added the number 1000 when a new local was chartered. This was an attempt to impress workers that a great many local unions were active across the country).

Then on March 2, 1937 the United States Steel Corporation shocked the country and the rest of the steel industry by signing a contract with the SWOC (See Appendix B-5 for a copy of the contract). The union was recognized, grievance procedures were established, wages were raised 10 percent, and seniority rights were established. Now that there was a victory in 'Big Steel' the SWOC was energized to organize 'Little Steel'. Little Steel was the five independent steel companies consisting of Republic, Youngstown Sheet and Tube, Inland, Bethlehem, and Weirton. The Little Steel companies, led by Tom Girdler of Republic, decided to fight the new union with all their energy. Girdler said, "I will go out and sell apples before I deal with the union."

To mobilize for the fight Republic ordered a large supply of guns and tear gas which were delivered to the Chicago plant as well as Republic mills in Ohio. Later a Senate investigation would find Republic Steel had purchased 550 revolvers, 65 rifles, 245 shotguns, 143 gas guns, 4000 gas projectiles, 2700 gas grenades, and a number of night sticks. Republic had bought more gas gun supplies than the entire Chicago Police Department. The SWOC knew this battle would have to be fought on the picket lines. From March, when the U.S. Steel contract was signed, until May, 1937 the SWOC attempted to negotiate a contract with Little Steel. A strike against 'Little Steel' was called for May 26, at 11 PM.

Steel Workers Attention!

"The Company Union Is Illegal!"

Such is the advice of the Company Union Lawyer to Employee Representatives of the United States Steel Corporation. At last the Bastard Monster which has no place in civilized America is declared officially Dead by its makers.

The Steel Workers' Union Drive Has Killed the Company Union
Now What?

The Forward March of Industrial Union for Steel Workers' Economic Security is on

No Power in America Can Stop It

Just as sure as Old Glory is the Flag of the Land just that sure the Amalgamated Association of Iron, Steel and Tin Workers of North America is the only Union of and for Steel Workers in the Country.

JOIN THIS UNION
JOIN THE FORWARD MARCH
STEEL WORKERS' ORGANIZING COMMITTEE

Flyer handed out by steelworker union organizers in late 1936 and early 1937.

First union picket line at Republic Steel (1937).

The Streets of Chicago

The union strategy at the Republic plant was: 1) The 11 PM shift would not go in. It was a strong union shift; 2) The 3 to 11 shift, also strongly sympathetic to the union, would strike the plant and walk out at about quitting time; 3) These two shifts, together, would keep the day shift (the union's weak point particularly in the mechanical trades) out the next day.

In the hours before the strike Superintendents and foreman told men on the day shift not to go home but to proceed to hiding places in the mill. During the afternoon shift management told known union men the strike had started early and they should walk out. Through trickery the company managed to confuse the men on the eve of the strike. Despite this 500 men walked out by 6 PM on May 26. The strikers attempted to set up a picket line in front of the gate but were met by 100 Chicago police. The police had been camped out in the mill cafeteria. They attacked the strikers' picket line and used their clubs, arresting 23.

The strikers decided to regroup and plan strategy and tactics. They established a headquarters in an old tavern known as Sam's Place which was located at 11317 Greenbay, six blocks from the plant headquarters (page 98). On May 28, the strikers attempted to establish a mass picket line in front of the main gate. They were attacked by police with the result of 16 men being hospitalized. Both Mayor Kelly and Police Commissioner Alman came under pressure to respond to these incidents on the picket line. The Mayor said that picketing was legal and the strikers could have as many as they wanted. The Police Commissioner said, "They can have all the pickets they want."

Taking the word of these city officials the strikers called a meeting for Sunday, Memorial Day, May 30 at Sam's place. Unknown to the SWOC the police had received information that strikers would attempt to invade the plant on Sunday and drive out non-union workers. As a result 265 police were ordered to the plant Sunday afternoon. Workers inside the plant were sleeping in the plant and using a partially finished wire mill as a dormitory. The stated purpose of the SWOC meeting was to establish a mass picket line in front of the plant. Pictures of this rally and of the strikers heading to the plant are shown on pages 99 and 100. As the meeting began at 3 PM it was clear and warm in Chicago. There was a picnic atmosphere among the 1500 present. Not only were there strikers present but family members and sympathizers from other mills. The meeting was addressed by Nickolas Fontecchio, SWOC District Director, and a former Mine Workers official. Leo Krzycki, on loan from the Amalgamated Clothing Workers, also spoke about the right of peaceful picketing.

As the speeches ended someone from the audience suggested a march to the main gate to establish a picket line. About two-thirds of the crowd started a march behind two American flags down Greenbay Avenue. They chanted, "CIO, CIO!" Participants walked to 114th street and then started down the dirt roads which led to the gate area. The dirt paths led through an area of prairie and open fields which was muddy

Union strike headquarters - Sam's Place (1937).

Rally before the Memorial Day march (1937).

Strikers and sympathizers head for plant (1937).

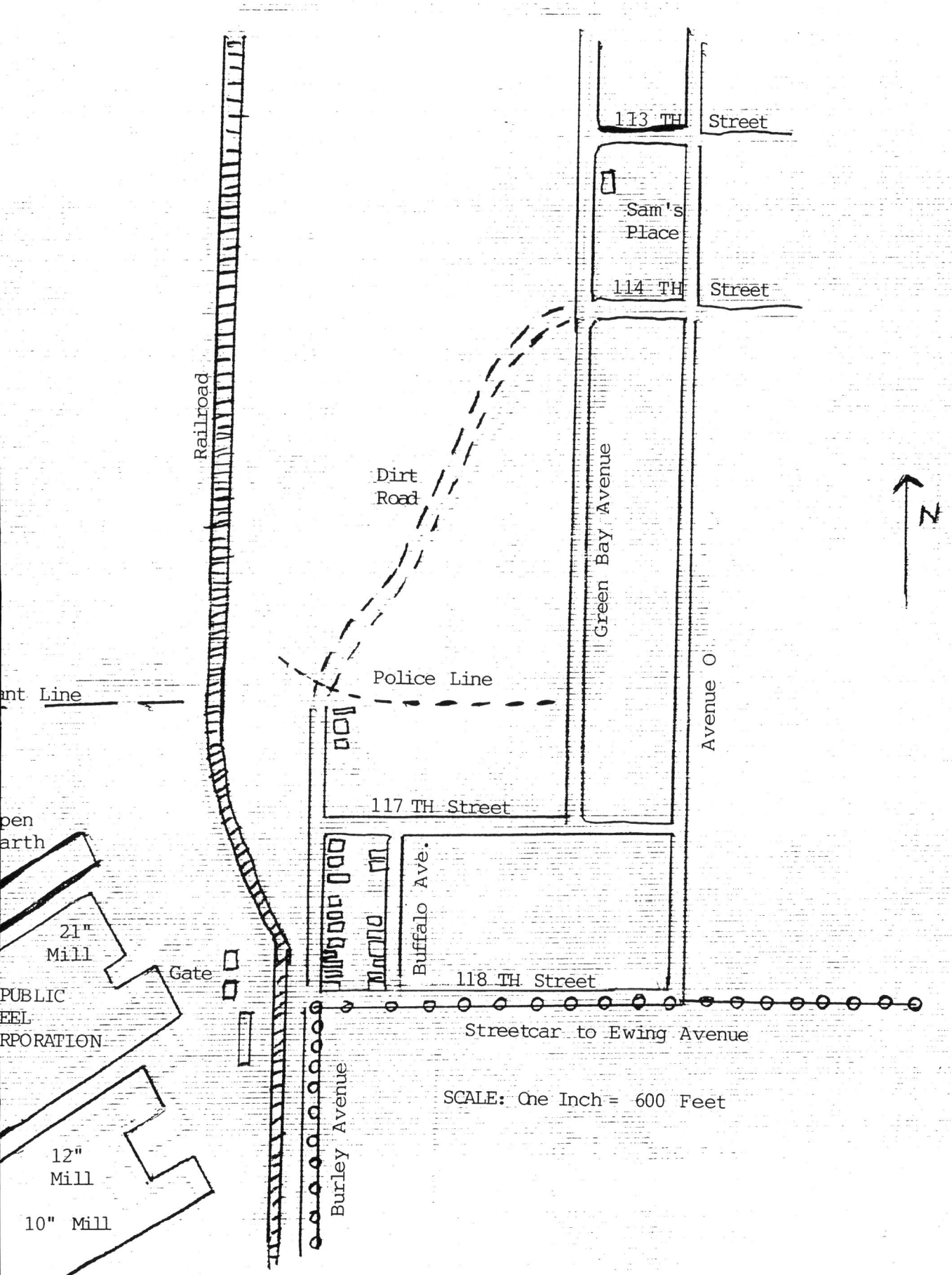

and litter-strewn. Many of the marchers carried picket signs denouncing Republic's labor policy or proclaiming the right to picket. The main body of police moved almost two blocks north to about 116th street to meet the marchers. The west edge of the 300 foot police line edged north to prevent the marchers from making a end run around the line (see Map page 101).

March leaders asked the police for permission to proceed to the gate to picket. The police refused and told them to disperse. The crowd was chanting union slogans and many were shouting at the police. Paramount Films had a cameraman recording the scene. Unfortunately the cameraman had to change his lens during the time the actual violence began. The cameraman estimated the lens changeover took about 7 seconds. The picture shown on the bottom of page 103 was taken when the film was not being recorded. This picture shows many of the marchers throwing various missiles and objects at the police. These objects were later identified as stones from slingshots, bolts and other pieces of metal. The police are trying to shield themselves from this attack. In previous accounts of the Massacre this particular picture has never been printed by pro-union writers.

One officer fired a warning shot in air and others drew their weapons. The missiles from the crowd continued. Tear gas canisters were thrown at the people standing on the east edge. Police in the rear began to fire in the air and police in the front drew their weapons and fired them at the crowd. The marchers fell back and fled in confusion and horror. People stumbled on top of one another as the police attack continued. In a 15 second period about 180 shots were fired by the police. Although newspapers reported at least one shot had been fired by someone in the crowd there was never any hard evidence of that.

The police line moved forward using their batons on marchers who had fallen or were wounded. Some police dragged marchers, wounded or not, dumping them into patrol wagons. The strikers retreated back to Sam's Place where wounded and injured were treated by doctors. When the bodies were counted four had been shot fatally with six more to die in the days to follow. Another 30 were wounded and dozens more hospitalized. Of the four dozen gunshot wounds four were frontal but most were back wounds. None of the police had been badly injured. The most serious was a broken arm and 30 others had cuts and bruises. One resident of the small group of houses and taverns near the Republic gate, Ann Dodaja, told this writer she saw a policeman who appeared to be shot in the face. She said after the police action the police would allow no one off streetcars unless they lived in the area.

The following strikers and supporters died: Hilding Anderson, age 29, died of blood poisoning from a wound; Alfred Causey, 43, killed by four bullet wounds; Leo Francisco, 17, died of a back wound; Earl Handley, 37, died of a hemorrhage when his wounds were not treated promptly; Otis Jones, 33, died of a bullet in the back; Sam Popovich, 50, died of a broken skull; Kenneth Reed, 23, bled to death in a patrol

Police await marchers as they head to plant.

This picture was taken while the newsreel camera was not operating. The picture has not been published in previous accounts of this incident. It shows the police in the foreground dodging a shower of missiles as the crowd advances. Apparently an overreaction to this provocation caused the police to fire their guns into the marchers.

Police club marchers.

Police follow marchers as they retreat to Sam's Place.

In these photographs police club helpless marchers, many of whom were wounded by gunfire.

Police would not allow proper medical attention to be given to those wounded.

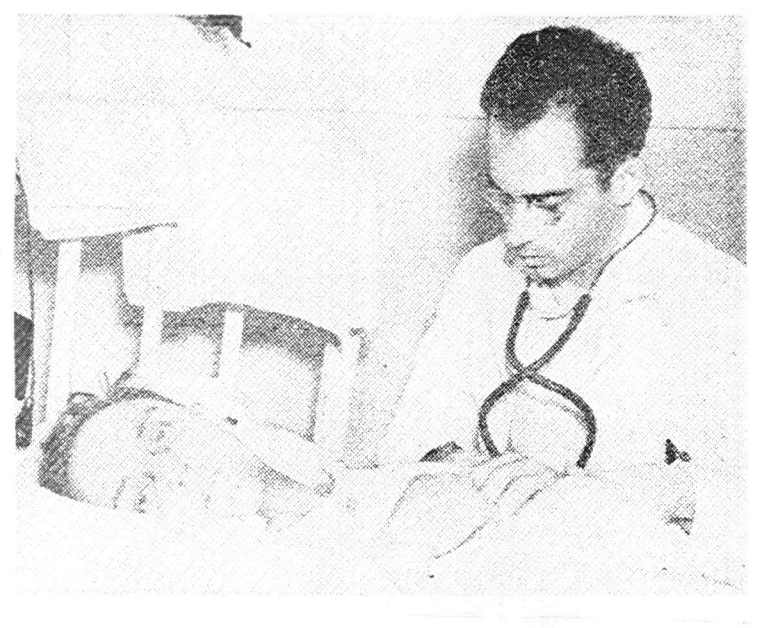

Hilding Anderson waged a grim fight for life at South Chicago Hospital following the massacre. He died shortly after to become one of the 10 men killed that day.

Five thousand strikers and sympathizers held a mass meeting at Washington Park in East Chicago, Indiana to protest the killings.

Speakers at the East Chicago protest rally. Speaking is (1) Nicholas Fontecchio, Calumet District Director of SWOC and standing at right (2) is Van A. Bittner, Regional Director. Besides Bittner is one of the strikers hurt in the battle.

wagon; Joseph Rothmund, 48, shot in the back; Anthony Tagliori, 26, the only Republic employee, was killed by a bullet in the back; and Lee Tisdale, 50, died of blood poisoning from a bullet wound. In addition during the Republic Steel strike two strikers were killed at the Republic mill in Youngstown, Ohio and four were killed at the Republic plant in Massillon, Ohio.

A United States Senate investigation of the violence questioned police actions in interfering with the picketing. It condemned the use of firearms. The Paramount Newsreel film was shown in the Senate and around the country. The film helped build support for the strikers but ironically it was not allowed to be shown in Chicago. The police film censorship board banned the film for many years.

The violence and anti-union feelings took its toll and the strike was called off in September, 1937. Republic refused to take back many of the union organizers. The SWOC filed a complaint with the National Labor Relations Board (NLRB). A long legal battle followed in the courts. Finally on August 13, 1942 the NLRB ordered Republic to negotiate a contract with the union. The company complied fearing loss of government war contracts. As part of the settlement Republic Steel was compelled to reinstate all active strikers to their former jobs with back pay of nearly $500,000. The steel company also paid $350,000 in damages to the injured and the families of the dead. During this time all the 'Little Steel" companies signed similar contracts. The many deaths in 1937 eventually resulted in union contracts for tens of thousands of workers.

The Memorial Day Massacre occurred when the police, fueled by rumors of plant invasion, were provoked by missiles being thrown at them. In addition, many of the police upon hearing their fellow officers shooting in the air, may have thought they were under fire. The police response was completely in excess of whatever provocation they faced. This was the bloodiest single labor battle in Chicago's history.

HONOR OUR DEAD

MURDERED by the Chicago Police for the Republic Steel Corporation on Memorial Day

Funeral Services

For Steel Union Martyrs at Eagles Hall, 9233 Houston Avenue

Thursday, June 3rd, at 2 P. M.

Bodies Will Lie in State from 10 a. m. to 2 p. m. 9233 Houston Ave.

JOIN THE UNION
JOIN THE PICKET LINE
Win the Cause They Gave Their Lives For

439   STEEL WORKERS ORGANIZING COMMITTEE

Union notice for funeral services for the five who died immediately.

POST WAR

RETREAT

5

RADICAL STRIKE AGAINST HARVESTER (1952)

As was seen in the resolution of the Little Steel contracts the War Labor Board (WLB) had great power to settle labor disputes. During World War II labor and management agreed there would be no strikes or lock-outs for the duration. Disputes were to be given to the WLB. These factors ensured very few major disputes during the War. The only exception to this in Chicago was the labor dispute involving the Montgomery Ward company. In 1942 Montgomery Ward had signed a contract with the Chicago local of the Retail, Wholesale and Department Store Workers when President Roosevelt enforced a WLB order. In 1944 Montgomery Ward refused to renew the contract and after a short strike Roosevelt ordered the company seized. Troops from the army were used to oust Ward's executives. The war ended before the legality of the seizure was settled.

During the time that the SWOC was organizing the mills in South Chicago a unit of the steelworker committee formed the Farm Equipment Workers Organizing Committee (FEWOC) in an attempt to organize the farm implement industry, specifically International Harvester. Company unions in the name of Works Councils had been used at Harvester to keep CIO type unions out of the plants. In 1937 the Supreme Court had ruled the Wagner Act made these company influenced unions illegal. International Harvester had two major plants in Chicago, McCormick Works and Tractor Works, both located on the near southwest side. Violence at a strike at McCormick Works had sparked the Haymarket riot in 1886. In 1938 workers at Tractor Works voted for representation by FEWOC. The FEWOC became the Farm Equipment Workers (FE) and in the next three years the FE drove the International Harvester company unions out of all company plants. In addition, the United Auto Workers (UAW) organized in International Harvester truck plants.

The FE established itself as an militant union. During World War II and afterwards many unions had espoused a spirit of cooperation with management. Many leaders

To the Public:
HERE IS THE REASON FOR THE HARVESTER STRIKE

FARM EQUIPMENT-UE has represented International Harvester workers for 15 years. On May 14 we sat down with the company representatives to negotiate wage increases and contract improvements.

There is no argument against workers needing higher pay. Government figures just released show the average city family had to go $400 in debt to make both ends meet in 1950—and it was far worse in 1951.

In three months of negotiations the Company countered every Union demand for higher wages with demands that the Union accept wage cuts. This is the same Company which, in moving its Twine Mill south, refuses even to consider the future of 865 faithful workers who have 10,000 years of IH seniority!

Can the Company afford wage increases? Let's look at the record:

1945—IH profits after taxes..$24,477,000

1948—IH profits after taxes..$55,679,000

1951—IH profits after taxes..$63,001,000

But the Company insisted on wage cuts! And they answered all Union demands for reasonable contract improvements with demands that the Union amend 60% of the old contract clauses in a manner favorable to Harvester.

PAY CUTS, PAY CUTS

On August 20, before negotiations collapsed, the Company notified several thousand employees that it was changing their job classifications. And here's what that meant—an actual example:

- George Skinner, an employee in Department 14 at the Chicago Tractor Works, with 32 years' service, was notified that he was being reclassified from Labor Grade 12 to Labor Grade 8. The first pays $2.17 an hour; the second pays only $1.89 an hour—a 28c pay cut!

- Skinner will continue to be paid his $2.17 as an "over-rate." But when he is promoted, transferred, or laid off, the new man going on the job will get only $1.89. This means widespread wage cuts. Thousands of men and women move up and down in Harvester's wage structure every year.

- The devaluation of thousands of jobs means a general lowering of the average wage. Nor will any of the "over-rates" get any of the increases negotiated by the Union. Skinner, suddenly an "over-rate," will not get an increase until the Union negotiates raises in excess of 28c hourly!

In addition to this wage-cutting program, the Company demanded contract clauses that permit daywork and piecework wages to be cut throughout the life of the contract at the Company's will.

Under such conditions, the Company would siphon back a so-called 4c production increase, as well as most or all of any cost-of-living adjustments.

The Harvester Company has made demands for over 1,000 classification and contract changes that would depress wages by over 30c an hour!

OTHER UNIONS HIT TOO

Such wage cuts have been put into effect in Harvester's Milwaukee plant (AFL) and in the plants under contract to the UAW-CIO. The cuts caused a long strike this year in the Milwaukee plant, and are the cause of the current UAW strike at Melrose Park.

All these strikes, ours included, are the last resort of working men and women who are determined to secure economic justice from a corporation which is sweating more and more production and profits out of its employees each year.

Productivity per worker increases at the rate of 16c per hour each year—not the 4c reflected in phoney productivity increases. (Industry sources.) In 1941 profit per Harvester worker was $1,060; in 1951 it was $2,532. (Company financial reports.)

REASONABLE UNION DEMANDS

Here are the Union demands as made May 14, and as they stand right now:

1. A 15c hourly general wage increase.
2. Elimination of the differences in pay between plants for the same work.
3. Adjustment of wage inequities, especially for skilled, day-rated, and office workers.
4. Real safeguards against wage cuts, job-price cuts, and speed-up.
5. Adequate health and welfare plan.
6. Safeguarding of the jobs of McCormick Twine Mill workers.
7. A liberalized vacation plan.
8. Better working conditions through more effective application of seniority, improved grievance procedure, and increased opportunities for promotions.
9. Withdrawal of Harvester's drastic contract proposals and rescinding of all recently announced wage cuts.

With the strike fully effective we resume negotiations this week. We are cooperating fully with the U. S. Government, through its Conciliation Service, to end the strike—with raises and contract improvements.

FARM EQUIPMENT-UE • NATIONAL HARVESTER CONFERENCE BOARD
UNITED ELECTRICAL, RADIO & MACHINE WORKERS OF AMERICA

GERALD FIELDE, Director, Harvester Conference Board
37 South Ashland Boulevard, Chicago 7, Ill.

UE International President, ALBERT FITZGERALD
11 East 51st Street, New York 22, N. Y.

Newspaper advertisement placed by the union to gain public support (1952).

Now – you may have a better idea of "Harvester's Labor Problem"

WE HAVE long been sensitive to the steady rash of news items about Harvester labor troubles. The seeming Communist line followed by certain union leaders has been one of which we have been long aware.

It is now out in the open as a result of testimony before the United States House of Representatives Committee on un-American activities, at hearings in Chicago. You may find in these Chicago newspaper headlines at least a partial answer to the frequent question asked by our friends and neighbors, "Why is there so much labor trouble at Harvester?"

As to the loyalty and fair-mindedness and decency of the great majority of our employes, we do not have the slightest doubt. However, we sincerely believe many of them are being misled by the leaders of the Farm Equipment Workers Council-United Electrical Workers. It is our belief, and has been for many years, that the most influential leaders of FE-UE are either Communists or Communist sympathizers and fellow travelers.

Under the circumstances, you may well ask:

"If the Company believes FE-UE to be a Communist-dominated union, why does the Company continue to deal with FE-UE?"

That is a proper question. The answer is:

Under the present labor laws of the United States we have no choice. FE-UE has been certified as bargaining agent for these units by the National Labor Relations Board. If we withdrew recognition from FE-UE we would probably be found guilty of an unfair labor practice under the law.

In short, we are compelled by law to recognize and deal with FE-UE and its leaders notwithstanding our beliefs about them.

INTERNATIONAL  HARVESTER

Newspaper advertisement placed by Harvester attacking communist ties to union.

Rally outside plant rally by strikers to denounce strikebreakers (1952).

Car driven by worker which was set afire by the strikers (1952).

of both AFL and CIO unions felt their membership could be more secure and gain more through company profitability. The FE attacked this philosophy. This union did not want wage increases tied to productivity. Harvester wanted restrictions on strikes and incentive tied to productivity. In the seven years after World War II Harvester plants represented by the FE had almost 1000 'wildcat' (unauthorized) strikes. Slowdowns as a means of dealing with grievances were also promoted by the FE. With the advent of the Cold War International Harvester decided to confront the union and use the fact it was led by political radicals to end it's representation in the plants. Harvester Chairman John McCaffrey told FE members the FE was led by "irresponsible radicals, who have no respect for their contracts, and who are more interested in disruption than in labor-management peace." He further said the company had good relations with 22 other international unions in it's plants.

In 1949 the CIO expelled the FE and 10 other communist dominated unions. Shortly before the expulsion, the FE had joined with the communist led United Electrical Workers (UE) and was sometimes known as FE-UE. Walter Reuther, head of the UAW, started to sign-up members (raids) at FE locals. Many plants went over to the UAW but the main Chicago plants remained in FE hands. At the beginning of summer, 1952, the UAW started another raid to free the FE members "from Moscow."

August, 1952, also saw International Harvester move it's Twine Mill to New Orleans from Chicago. The FE organized actions within the plant to stop machinery from being moved out. Harvester shut the plant and the FE placed this issue as part of contract negotiations. The company put forward it's own list of demands which restricted union activity. The FE struck Harvester on August 21, 1952. Chicago plants provided 15,000 of the 30,000 who walked out. As the strike progressed both the company and union used newspaper ads to attack each other (see pages 112 and 113). Picket line fights took place daily. Bricks were thrown through the windows of workers crossing the line. Some cars were burnt along Western Avenue. In an effort to stop the violence police made scores of arrests in the streets around the factories.

Three weeks after the strike began violence started against nonstrikers. On September 15 Watson Wright was bludgeoned with a baseball bat and suffered a fractured skull. On October 3 William Foster died from a beating as he walked to work. The Financial Secretary of the FE, Harold Ward, was charged in both these cases. Due to these incidents and others, Harvester was able to get a court injunction in mid-October which limited picketing to six at each gate. This injunction was the beginning of the end for the FE strike. Many strikers went back to work and the FE signed a contract on November 15, 1952 which included all of Harvester's demands for wage revisions and union restrictions. Before the expiration of the three year contract the FE locals at Harvester left the FE-UE and merged with the UAW. The labor battles which began at McCormick Works in 1886 ended when International Harvester shut the factory down in 1959.

STEEL INDUSTRY AND UNION IN TRANSITION (1970S)

By the end of the 1950s there was almost 10,000 manufacturing plants within the Chicago city limits and 14,000 in the metropolitan area. This area led the nation in the manufacture of steel, electrical and non-electrical machinery, radio and television sets, tin cans, fabricated metal products, cosmetics, non-metallic minerals, and food processing. Competition, technology, and geography would soon change those industrial rankings. The packinghouses moved closer to cattle raising in the west, Foreign competition overwhelmed much of clothing, electronics, autos, farm equipment, and basic steel. After McCormick Works and Tractor Works shut down they were jointed by Campbell Soup, Zenith, Wisconsin Steel, Pullman Standard, the Hawthorne plant of Western Electric, U.S. Steel and Republic/LTV Steel. In the 35 years following World War II Chicago lost 60 percent of its manufacturing jobs.

The steel industry in Chicago was typical of the fortunes of heavy industry. Chicago was part of the Calumet steel district which included mills in NE Illinois and NW Indiana. Major mills in the area included U.S. Steel Gary Works, Inland Steel, Youngstown Sheet and Tube, Republic Steel, U.S. Steel South Works, Bethlehem Steel, and Interlake Steel. In the 1980s LTV Steel took over Republic and Youngstown while Interlake became ACME Steel. The output of these mills in the late 1970s was over 30 million tons annually, far above the Pittsburgh area.

The Steelworkers Union District 31 which represented the Calumet area was also the union's biggest district. It's membership jumped from 18,000 in 1937 at the time of the Little Steel strike to 100,000 in 1945 and it remained at 125,000 until the end of the 1970s. District 31 had been led by District Director Joseph Germano from 1942 until 1973 when he faced mandatory retirement at age 65. An election was held in February, 1973 between Ed Sadlowski and Samuel Evett. Evett had been Germano's assistant for many years and was the choice of the International leadership in Pittsburgh. Sadlowski, who ran on a platform of reform, had been President of the U.S. Steel local in South Chicago and was on the USWA staff. Evett won the election by 1700 out of 45,000 votes cast. Sadlowski charged vote fraud took place in some of the basic steel locals and the U.S. Department of Labor agreed and overturned the election. A new election was held and Sadlowski was successful by a wide margin (see page 117). In 1977 Sadlowski ran against Lloyd McBride for International President. Although he won the United States vote by a small margin he lost big in Canada and was defeated. There was some violence in the election but it was minor compared to some other unions.

Starting in the late 1970s the steel industry in Chicago and nationally went into a tail spin. In 1980 Wisconsin Steel shut down. In 1982 much of U.S. Steel South Works shut down. This was followed by Republic/LTV Steel in 1986. All of these mills were within blocks of one another on the SE side of the city. This had a devastating effect on the area economy. This mirrored what was happening elsewhere in Chicago

Voice of the RANK & FILE

Vol. 25   "THE NEWSPAPER DEDICATED TO WORKING FOR THE WORKERS."   November, 1973

DIST. DIR. ELECTION OVERTURNED

Widespread Vote Fraud Uncovered

On Monday, November 5, 1973, the U.S. Department of Labor ordered the election of February 13, 1973, for the office of District 31 Director be set aside and a new election be held. A new election to be conducted under the supervision of the Federal Government for the 130,000 steelworkers in Northern Illinois and Indiana was called for because of excessive irregularities in the original election.

The government order grew out of charges of vote fraud brought by Ed Sadlowski, a candidate for District 31 Director, after the International Union of the U.S.W.A. failed to act on his charges.

Election results, released by the U.S.W.A. on April 16, 1973 showed Sadlowski trailing Samuel Evett by about 1700 votes of almost 45,000 votes cast. District 31 is the largest District among 24 in the U.S. and Canada.

"I feel the Government's action today upholds my claim of victory and unfair campaign practices and widespread voting irregularities on election day," commented Sadlowski.

"I believe the 130,000 steelworkers in District 31 have been dealt a serious injustice--an injustice I sincerely hope will be quickly remedied," added Sadlowski.

Sadlowski had issued warnings weeks before election day that his campaign was not being provided the necessary information as required by the USWA's constitution and election bylaws. Immediately following the announcement of the election results, he filed a protest with the International Union of USWA, challenging vote fraud and other irregularities in various local unions in District 31.

Among some of charges lodged by Sadlowski were:

1. Forging of members signatures on voting roster by Election Tellers in Local 1066, Gary, Indiana.
2. Stuffing of ballot boxes.
3. Use of Union funds and properties to promote the candidacy of Samuel Evett.
4. Refusing to allow Sadlowski's observers to monitor casting and counting of ballots.
5. Failure to provide locations of voting places and hours of voting to permit assignment of Sadlowski observers.
6. Holding no elections in some locals.
7. Failure to properly post notices of elections among the membership.

"There was never any question in my mind, or my supporters, that I had won the election," said Sadlowski. "I think it is sad that my challenge had to go to the Federal Government. I would have much preferred that the Union clean its own house. Recognition of one's right to a secret ballot and an honest and fair election is sacred and I think it is high time that the stagnant bureaucrats who lead the Steelworkers Union realize it."

"I based my campaign on the recognition of the worth of each Union member," continued Sadlowski. "I believe we need Union Leaders who listen, respect and respond to the needs of the membership."

District 31 members work in about 400 plants located in a 10-county area which forms the Lake Michigan basin. The International Union represents about 1.5 million steelworkers throughout the United States and Canada. The district directorship was vacated by the retirement of Joe Germano, who had held the position for 34 years. Germano had publicly announced his support for Evett, his long-time assistant.

Sadlowski, 35 years of age, is a staff member of the International Union and was twice elected president of Local Union 65, the largest local in Illinois, which serves the 8,000 members working in U.S. Steel South Works in South Chicago. Sadlowski became the first person to contest the position in more than 25 years, when he garnered more than double the number of nominations required to run for the office.

LOCAL 1010 CONDEMNS GOON TACTICS

The recent mistreatment of a Local 1010 delegate, Lyon Leifer, at the union's District Conference on October 13, was condemned in a resolution passed at the Local meeting of November 1. The resolution, which was proposed by the executive board and passed unanimously in a floor vote, demands that District Director Sam Evett carry out a speedy investigation of the charge that a number of Sargents at Arms of the District Conference seized Brother Leifer for no cause, roughed him up and ejected him from the proceedings of the Conference.

Brother Leifer, a Griever Steward in area 22 (No. 3 OH, Mold Foundry, Electric Shop) and a member of the Rank and File Caucus, told "The Voice of the Rank and File" that the reason he was treated so badly was that he and another delegate to the Conference were trying to use their democratic right to disagree with the top leadership's signing of the no-strike agreement. He also said, "I want to thank all the brothers and sisters who've expressed their indignation over the treatment I received from those goons. I also want to thank the executive board of the local for reporting favorably on my protest. Unless we oppose goon squad tactics the moment they appear, as we have done now, the situation for democracy in our union is bound to get even worse than it is today. Every member must have the right to take a stand on the issues facing our union and to win the membership to his or her side if that position is correct."

MEET & HEAR

ED SADLOWSKI

SAT. NOV. 17th - 7:00 P.M.

SS. Peter & Paul Church
Columbus Dr. & Elm
Rank & File Smoker

Newsletter distributed to steel mills describing the USWA District Director election which was overturned (1973).

industry. The next labor battle in the Chicago would take place when new technology disrupted the existing workplace structure.

CHICAGO TRIBUNE STRIKE (1985)

Printers are the oldest trade union in Chicago. The Chicago Typographical Union Local 16 was formed in 1852. This was five years after the *Chicago Tribune* started publishing in 1847. At the time Chicago was attempting to gain business by working for a connecting waterway between the Great Lakes and the Mississippi River. The *Chicago Tribune* editorialized towards this goal which was achieved in April, 1848 when the Illinois and Michigan Canal was opened. Cryus McCormick, inventor of the grain reaper, visited Chicago looking for a location to build a reaper plant. He found an ideal location on the north side of the Chicago River, east of what is now Michigan Avenue (where the *Tribune* headquarters is now located). He built the McCormick Reaper Works, and was soon turning out hundreds of reapers each year.

In 1885 Joseph Medill became editor of the paper and he and a group of other individuals purchased the *Tribune*. Under his guidance the paper prospered and became influential in state and national politics. A nephew of Cryus McCormick married Medill's daughter and they had a son named Robert R. McCormick "The Colonel". The Colonel reigned over the *Chicago Tribune* for almost 40 years until his death in 1955. When he died his will tied up the paper in a complicated trust which diminished the effectiveness of management for 20 years. When the trust expired in 1975 the Tribune company found itself with financial problems not only at the *Chicago Tribune* but also the Tribune owned New York Daily News and their newsprint plants.

Facing these difficulties the Tribune asked the Typographical Union for concessions. In 1975 in return for lifetime job security the union agreed to give up jurisdictional rights over job duties. Over the next few years the Tribune began to press for Printers to be transferred into other bargaining units. In 1983 the Tribune introduced the Freedom Center which was their new technology driven printing center. Freedom Center cost $180 million and was the nation's most advanced newspaper printing operation. Since Freedom Center came on line the *Tribune*'s annual profit has gone from an average of 7 percent of operating costs to 25 percent. This printing plant was the result of a computerized trend which began sweeping the industry in the 1970s. Computerized photocomposition had reduced the ranks of union printers from 100,000 at the high point in the late 1960s to 40,000 by 1985.

Workers whose jobs were being eliminated were permitted to volunteer for new jobs outside their workplace. Since the Printers were the hardest hit by the new processes they were the most eager to transfer out. Nineteen printers had found work in other company departments and 51 others were signed up to transfer. The Tribune began bringing in new management from their Florida operations. George D. Veon was hired as Director of Employee Relations. He was known as someone experienced in newspaper strikes. Then in 1983 the Tribune suddenly ended the transfer program with the demand these workers renounce their union membership. The unions had basic control over hiring, through the "Call Room" where printers could hire temporary substitutes if they were not going to be present. The Tribune wanted this eliminated and they wanted to be able to hire more minorities. In late 1984 the company posted work rules. This posting stated:

1) **Only one doorway into and out of the work area. Other entrances would be locked.**

2) **Permission had to be given by one of the foreman, to permit a worker to go to the vending machines.**

3) **The workers had to report directly to the foreman in charge.**

4) **Security guards would randomly stop employees to search lunch boxes and underarm bags.**

When this notice was posted the number of wash rooms was reduced from five to one. This would be used by 75 to 80 employees a shift. These new conditions were intended to provoke a strike but the union waited.

Tribune management then chose Leonard Maslowski, the bottom man on the printers seniority list as a test case. He was assigned to be trained as a Mailer. The company was trying to set the precedent of a member of one union assigned to the work area of another union, and be assigned to an apprentice level. The unions felt this could not be tolerated. Who would be transferred next? Perhaps a group of older workers or some who had physical handicaps. The final blow came four days before the strike was called. Pressmen in the Freedom Center plant were herded into the lunchroom area by armed security guards using guard dogs.

Four days later, on a warm evening in July, 1985, the leaders of each union discreetly entered the work area of the workers on that shift and quietly instructed them to gather their personal belongings and exit the building. The management had gotten their way. A strike had, at long last, been called. One thousand workers, members of three production unions, walked out, and most would never return.

Tribune company owners felt they could not tolerate the work rules and past practices of nine different craft unions in the same shop. Contract negotiations were extensive with the three most prominent unions. Unions had charged the paper with stalling and attempting to provoke the strike. The Printers had met with the Tribune for over 2 years, the Mailers for 13 months, and the Pressmen for four months. The three key issues in dispute were job transfers, hiring, and union pensions.

WHY

SHOULD A RETIRED PERSON, A STUDENT OR ANY WORKER WHO IS NOT A MEMBER OF ANY UNION SUPPORT THE UNIONS STRIKING THE CHICAGO TRIBUNE?

- The unions have fought for many years for the rights of ALL of the people, union and nonunion.
- The benefits and better living standard enjoyed by ALL Americans have been obtained over many years of struggle by the unions.
- The unions have helped improve the Social Security system for EVERYONE. The greedy corporations now want to cut back on Social Security so they can add to the billions of dollars they are pocketing at the expense of the elderly.
- The unions fight for better educational systems and more grants for those needing money to go to college.
- The cutting back on hospitalization benefits will speed up the closing of more hospitals and cause the layoffs of hospital employees.
- If the corporations such as The Chicago Tribune are successful in breaking the unions, it means the next step will be to start cutting the benefits of the nonunion workers in every walk of life and in every type of job. No job will be safe. With nonunion wages slashed, your way of life will change.

THE TRIBUNE STRIKE IS NOT OVER TECHNOLOGY OR MONEY. IT IS JUST GREEDY OLD FASHIONED UNION-BUSTING AS WAS DONE IN THE EARLY 1900s. THE TRIBUNE IS A BILLION DOLLAR CORPORATION. THE UNIONS WANT A SIMPLE CONTRACT THEY CAN LIVE WITH. THE TECHNOLOGY ISSUE IS A SMOKE SCREEN FOR THE REAL CAUSE.

WITH YOUR SUPPORT WE CAN KEEP AMERICA FROM GOING BACK TO THE JUNGLE OF THE OLD DAYS. IT CAN'T HAPPEN? THAT IS JUST ABOUT WHEN IT WILL HAPPEN.

WE ASK YOUR HELP. WE ASK THAT YOU CANCEL YOUR TRIBUNE SUBSCRIPTION OR QUIT BUYING IT. USE THE ALTERNATIVE NEWSPAPERS AVAILABLE.

THE LACK OF CIRCULATION IS A POWERFUL REASON TO SETTLE.

This notice was distributed through out the Chicago area in an effort to gain support for a boycott of the *Tribune* (1985).

The union was active in promoting the boycott with demonstrations at *Tribune* headquarters and Wrigley Field (owned by the Tribune company).

The unions and the Chicago Federation of Labor launched a consumer boycott of the *Tribune*. They sent letters to 450,000 union households. The key to the strike became the Teamsters' Union. Their members drove the trucks which delivered the papers in the Chicago area. The Typographical Union had been in merger discussions with the Teamsters and were expected to join the powerful union in August. The printers fully expected the Teamsters to respect the picket lines. They did not. In an interview with this writer, Steve Berman current President of the Typographical local, said the strike was a mistake given the refusal of the Teamsters to honor the lines. The printers rejected the proposed merger once the drivers crossed the picket lines, The printers have since joined the Communication Workers of America.

In the immediate aftermath of the strike the *Tribune* had fewer pages, fewer editions, no color graphics or color photos in its news sections. Within weeks the paper was back to normal. The boycott had some success but not enough to get productive negotiations started. On January 30, 1986 the unions made an unconditional offer to return to work but none were recalled. In the meantime all the unions filed National Labor Relations Board complaints as well as lawsuits. These proceeded very slowly.

In late 1988 the Printers voted to end the strike and allow the paper to install a new position of typographical associate which would be paid a lower rate than the printer position. A final settlement was made in May, 1989 when a court consent decree was signed. This decree covered 240 original strikers. At the time 119 remained out and based on age and seniority they received buyouts between $30,000 and $90,000. At the paper 47 printers remained and they could stay or receive a $30,000 buyout. The rest had found other work, moved, or died. The *Chicago Sun-Times* introduced contract provisions in 1989 cutting printer pay by 40 percent. An arbitrator reversed the pay cut but allowed the paper the right to hire (instead of through the union) and gave it jurisdictional relief. Some court actions involving the Mailers and Pressmen remain to this day.

ORGANIZATION

IN THE

PUBLIC SECTOR

6

CHICAGO TEACHERS UNION

After World War II labor strife in the private sector of Chicago declined. Major industrial plants and factories which were the easiest to organize, had been. Of course many of those same factories had left Chicago and took the union jobs with them. Concurrently local and state government units greatly expanded their activity in Chicago. With this expansion came several attempts to organize the public sector. Previously many government leaders had saw unions and contracts as a threat to patronage. Legal and political assaults on the patronage system made union organizing much easier in the late part of the 20th century.

Financing of the public schools has always been a matter of controversy in Chicago. In 1845 the first permanent school (Dearborn) was built by the city at State and Madison. Mayor Garrett said it was "such an extravagance" that it should be turned into a insane asylum for the purpose of incarcerating those responsible for its erection. The graphic below shows how the Chicago School Board tried to maintain great control over teachers work and personal life.

Typical teacher duties in 1872:

- Each day fill lamps, clean chimneys

- Bring bucket of water and scuttle of coal.

- "Make your pens carefully. You may whittle nibs to the individual taste of pupils."

- Men teachers may take one evening each week for courting purposes, or two evenings a week if they go to church regularly.

- After 10 hours in schools, the teacher may spend remaining time reading the Bible or other good books.

- Women teachers who marry or engage in unseemly conduct will be dismissed.

- Every teacher should lay aside each pay day a goodly sum for his declining years, so that he will not become a burden on society.

- Any teacher who smokes, uses liquor, frequents pool or public halls, or gets shaved in a barber shop, will give good reasons to suspect his worth.

- The teacher who performs duties faithfully and without fault for 5 years will be given a 25 cents a week raise, if the Board approves.

The Streets of Chicago

In 1880 a School Board regulation dictated that the marriage of any female teacher was deemed equivalent to her resignation.

Perhaps because of these restrictions Chicago teachers were among the first group of workers organized in Chicago. The Chicago Teachers Federation (CTF) was formed on March 16, 1897, by teachers who were concerned the state legislature would not honor their commitment to the new pension program which had been passed in 1895. This was the first teachers' union in the nation and over half of Chicago teachers became members by the end of 1897. Margaret Haley, a teacher union activist, took five major utility and street railway companies to court for failure to pay taxes. The School Board had claimed an inability to pay for salary increases and Haley found that these major corporations were evading taxes on their franchises. The court action was successful and the companies paid $1 million to the schools. Haley became the leader of the CTF, which consisted primarily of women elementary teachers, in 1900 (see Haley's "Why Teachers Should Organize" in Appendix B-4). Under her leadership the CTF became the nation's most militant teachers organization. She fought to advance the cause of public education and the well-being of elementary school teachers in Chicago.

In 1902 the CTF affiliated with the Chicago Federation of Labor. In the next few years the School Board became increasingly concerned with Haley and the CTF's activities with Chicago's labor movement. In 1915 the School Board passed a rule outlawing affiliation of teachers with organized labor. The School Board President fired 68 activists who belonged to the CTF. The organizing that took place in order to get these teachers rehired resulted in the founding of the American Federation of Teachers in 1916. Under attack from the School Board the CTF gave up it's affiliation with organized labor in 1917.

By 1930 there were 25 teacher organizations in Chicago. The financial crisis of the Depression caused wage cuts and uncashable paychecks (see next page for a picture of a 1934 demonstration at City Hall). In 1937 four major teacher organizations merged to form the Chicago Teachers Union (CTU). At the end of one year the CTU had signed 70 percent of the Chicago's public school teachers. This was easily the largest teachers' union in the nation. During the ensuing years the CTU focused it's efforts on lobbying the legislature, court cases, and acting as a voice for the teachers with the School Board.

It would not be until 1964 that the CTU would be able to win a "Memorandum of Understanding" for "orderly and speedy processing" of grievances and professional problems. The CTU was still not the sole bargaining unit for Chicago teachers. That came in 1966 when the CTU won collective bargaining buy gaining 90 percent of the vote. The School Board recognized the CTU as the sole and exclusive bargaining agent for teachers, playground teachers, truant officers and assistant principals. In November, 1966 bargaining began on the first contract. The CTU House of Delegates

Teachers demonstrate outside City Hall in 1934 to protest payless paydays (CHS).

gave the School Board a December 15 deadline to adopt the union's monetary demands to avoid a work stoppage. In January, 1967 Mayor Daley intervened to avert a strike. The first contract made Chicago's teachers among the highest paid on the nation. It also contained a grievance procedure, established an average class size, and allowed union meetings which could be conducted on school time.

Two years later, May 1969, the CTU called the first teachers' strike in Chicago. The strike was 85 percent effective. The union sought no layoffs of teachers, maintain class size, no cutbacks in school programs, and a pay raise. This strike was successful after two days. In the early 1970s the CTU engaged in a series of strikes to win new contract gains and protect old ones. In December, 1979, school finances had hit a crisis point and teachers had their first payless payday since 1931. The School Board attempted to get the teacher's pension fund to lend the Board money but the CTU blocked that effort. After three consecutive payless paydays the Union struck for 10 days in January, 1980. The legislature engineered a bailout plan which included a School Finance Authority (SFA). The SFA had the authority to oversee School Board budgets which were required to be balanced. During the mid-1980s the union called three strikes lasting a total of 27 days. The main issues were pay and medical benefits. In 1987 the School Board attempted a 2 percent pay cut which provoked the longest strike in CTU history. After 19 days the union gained a 4 percent pay raise in each of the next two years.

In 1990 an interim School Board, appointed by Mayor Daley, and the CTU signed an early settlement for a three year contract, which contained a 21 percent pay raise, however the Board did not have adequate political backing to fund the agreement. This pact led to continued financing problems through the early 1990s. In 1993 the Mayor asked for concessions for the first time. The state legislature increasingly began to inject itself into the collective bargaining process. As part of the 1993 package Springfield passed a measure calling for work rules to be changed.

In 1995 the legislature passed a law abolishing the School Board, banning strikes for 18 months, banned class size as a matter for collective bargaining, and subject teachers to dismissal if there were adverse changes at their school. The new Board hired private teaching firms to go into the city schools and teach. Finally in 1996 the legislature considered a proposal which would order merit pay based on skill and performance to be part of the contract.

No matter what the present financial condition forces on the teachers and the CTU, the union has won great benefits for Chicago teachers. Before the first contract teachers were paid little, had no benefits, and it took teachers 36 years to reach the maximum salary. Union battles brought individual and then family hospitalization, seniority rights, paid vacations, teacher assistants, class sizes, sick days, a teacher supply allowance, pensions, and a grievance procedure.

BROTHERS OF THE BARREL - THE FIRE FIGHTERS STRIKE (1980)

The International Association of Fire Fighters was formed in the early 1900s. Chicago was chartered as Local 2 and became the nation's largest when the local in New York withdrew. For many years it was a social organization. During the 1970s the fire department started to make changes and modernize. In 1974 some police were caught taking bribes to take bodies to certain funeral homes. Mayor Daley was upset at this revelation and the city decided to hire paramedics to handle medical emergencies and body removal. Due to the end of the Vietnam War there were quite a number of ex-medics available. The first paramedic unit was formed which was a 'Call and Haul' group with no medical training. From the beginning there was division in the department. There was no incentive for firemen to take paramedic training. By learning paramedic duties the firemen would not get extra money -- just extra work. The paramedics were kept separate from the fire fighters union and there was a separate hiring list and pension fund.

In 1977 the union began to agitate for a written contract. Union members of the Chicago Fire Department had always had a "handshake" agreement with Mayor Richard J. Daley. There were no promotional exams and advancement in the department depended on the political clout of the fireman's "chinaman." When Daley died in late 1976 the union, Chicago Fire Fighters Local 2, decided it was time for a written contract. On May 1, 1978 Frank Muscare, a contract proponent, took office as President of Local 2. In August, 1978, Muscare and the union's executive board approved the draft of a contract and they adopted the slogan, "No more handshakes -- contract time 1979." For the rest of the year the union negotiating team met each Monday in the Bismarck Hotel awaiting representatives of the Bilandic administration to begin bargaining. Those officials never showed. In October Muscare attempted to gain a strike authorization vote. Rank and file members rejected the request 1729 - 1664. A city budget was adopted without contracts for firemen.

The union wrote a letter to mayoral candidate Jane Byrne asking for her support for a collective bargaining agreement. She expressed her support for a contract with fire fighters and other city workers. In her response Byrne agreed to six men per truck, and that seniority would govern in promotions and transfers, and she supported union recognition for all employees of the Department except civilians. The Fire Fighters union was the only union to endorse Byrne although they doubted that she could win.

Jane Byrne won the Democratic primary in an upset in February, 1979. After she took office she promised to begin talks with Muscare. In August her administration told the union talks would have to wait until the city council adopted a collective bargaining ordinance. The Firefighters asked the Fraternal Order of Police to have joint negotiations. This was rejected by the FOP. Union leaders began to meet weekly at the Bismarck Hotel but the Byrne administration refused to attend. There were issues which the Firefighters negotiating team wanted to discuss with the city. The six person team had one paramedic, Larry Matkaitis. This team wanted promotions to be handled fairly with no politics involved. Manning was a problem. The Chicago Fire Department often had four men per truck instead of five. Firemen were reassigned out of classification instead of others being brought in for overtime. The team wanted a health and safety committee. Medics wanted to be part of the same pension plan and be treated equally with the firemen. In late November frustrated union leaders asked the membership for a strike authorization vote. On December 16, 1979 the members approved a strike 2326 to 658. One thousand members did not vote.

On January 8, 1980 the city and union held their first contract meeting. The union called for a walkout at 5:30 AM on February 3. This was called off the day before the deadline when the city agreed that a fire contract would take precedence over a general bargaining ordinance. A city-wide teachers strike, which lasted two weeks, over the issue of payless paydays had started on February 4 which distracted city negotiators. Four days later the firefighter talks were declared at an impasse. Mayor Byrne said anyone who struck would be fired immediately. This inflamed firemen. To the union the main dispute was who would be covered by the contract and whether officers would be excluded. Muscare offered to exclude the Commissioner and his three deputies but wanted the union to represent all other uniformed firefighters, including chiefs, captains, and lieutenants. The next day, February 8, the union offered to send the dispute to a mediation. On February 13 marathon sessions with state and federal mediators broke off at 2:15 AM and the union authorized Muscare to set a time for the strike. The next day, Valentine's Day, at 5:15 AM firemen walked off their jobs.

In the week before the strike the city had taken a survey of fire houses asking members if they would walkout. Most lied to the survey takers and said they would not. The city felt they could operate with 950 men. A normal 24 hour shift has 1100 men working. The city was taken by surprise when 96 percent of firemen walked out. The union had offered the city a contingency plan where striking firemen would respond to calls and fight fires. This is known as a silver-spanner strike. The city rejected the plan saying this would turn the fire department over to the union. The fire department turned off the repeater radios denying the union's ability to hear where the fires were. William Quinlan, chief corporation counsel, went to the kitchen of Circuit Court Judge John Hechinger, and delivered an affidavit by Fire Commissioner Richard Albrecht stating a general walkout had began. Hechinger signed a temporary order banning the strike. There was no state law prohibiting public workers from striking. The only precedent was case law (on garbage drivers in another city). Albrecht canceled all furloughs and days off and ordered night shift firemen to remain on duty. This order was largely ignored. Albrecht asked for double the police protection at fire stations and said "We will surround every firehouse with policemen".

Astro, mascot of Snorkel No. 1 joins pickets outside firehouse at 55 E. Illinois St.

Sign at the Fire Fighters Daley Plaza rally.

The Streets of Chicago

Talks resumed the next day with a federal mediator. When they broke off after 14 hours the city asked Hechinger for contempt citations. Judge Hechinger was a union representative for the cemetery workers before he became a judge. He thought the demand for a contract was reasonable. Hechinger tried to mediate the dispute and the talks resumed for a short time. Later, Hechinger warned the union to report to work by 10 AM the next day or face contempt. Mayor Byrne warned the strikers they would be fired if they did not report. The next day, February 17, firemen refused to report and 500 demonstrated in Daley Plaza (see picture page 130). Hechinger imposed a $40,000 daily fine on the union and its leaders for refusing to end the strike. On February 18 the city started to hire recruits and Mayor Byrne said she, "will never negotiate" with Muscare.

On February 20, during a court session, the union agreed to send their members back to work while 24 hour around the clock negotiations are conducted. Issues to be negotiated were to be: 1) truck manning - the union wanted a specific number and the city wanted flexibility; 2) job seniority - the union wanted this to govern promotions and transfers, the city said no; and 3) union recognition - the union wanted everyone except the top four commissioners, the city did not want anyone at covered at the rank of lieutenant or above. The union insisted on amnesty for all strikers but Mayor Byrne refused amnesty for any union members accused of criminal conduct. The city wanted Muscare out of further negotiations and went after him for criminal contempt. As an excuse they said Muscare had ordered the firemen to bring back their picket signs inside the fire houses. Hechinger, appalled at the city's attitude, went to city hall to plead for reasonableness. He was told by Byrne that unless he jailed Muscare he would not be re-slated for election. When he came back to Daley Center observers thought it looked like he had been slugged. Hechinger told Muscare "I will do what I have to do." Muscare said, "She cut your balls off." Larry Matkaitis was standing in the back of the courtroom with a radio. Hechinger sentenced Muscare to five months in jail for criminal contempt of court. The judge also fined Muscare and 11 other union leaders. Matkaitis radioed Bill Reddy, the union's First Vice President, and he ordered the firemen back out of the fire houses.

Over the next few days the CFL, the fire fighters union, and the city met and worked out a "memorandum of agreement." The main remaining issue was amnesty. On February 28 Commissioner Albrecht issued an ultimatum to fire fighters to return to work by 8 PM or face disciplinary action. Very few went to Navy Pier to sign up for work.

On March 1 Mayor Byrne vowed to reorganize the Fire Department and said she was opposed to amnesty for all strikers. She said the city would hire 200 more recruits which would bring to 1132 the number of recruits in training or on the job. Byrne said the city would fire 274 strikers. On March 5 the union membership voted down a back-to-work plan offered by the city. This proposal came after Byrne met with Frank Palumbo, an official of the International Association of Fire Fighters. On March 6

Mayor Byrne denounced the strike as a "political strike" encouraged by her foe, State Sen. Richard M. Daley.

Edward Kennedy, who was running for President in the Democratic primary, made a speech with Byrne at the Hilton on February 29. The union surrounded the Hilton in order to embarrass Byrne who was backing Kennedy. Kennedy called Byrne and told her he did not want a labor demonstration on St. Patricks Day. He had planned to march in the parade right before the primary on March 18. The mayor appointed Rev. Jesse Jackson, head of Operation PUSH, as a mediator in the dispute. Jackson had met with 60 Black fire fighters on February 25 to press demands for affirmative action and representation in the union. There were 425 Black fire fighters and all but 50 had joined the strike. On March 7, after 12 hours of talks, Rev. Jackson said an agreement had been reached. In the talks Jackson had told the union that 400 Black firemen "were ready to move." If the union did not settle they could expect to see the Blacks go back in. The agreement was approved by the city council executive committee. On Saturday, March 8 at 1:40 AM, the fire fighters voted unanimously to end the strike and return to work later that day. The union gave up its demand for total amnesty, agreeing that every striker will lose a day's pay and striking battalion chiefs will lose four days' pay. A measure of affirmative action had been agreed to. The city would hire 800 more Blacks and 500 Hispanics in the Fire Department.

The agreement called for a package of unresolved issues to be arbitrated. The union won most issues in arbitration. Only 60 people out of 4350 were excluded from the bargaining unit. Manning for fire trucks was won by the union with five per truck. A promotional career ladder was agreed to. Paramedics went into the pension fund in 1983. A new grievance procedure with arbitration was part of the new contract. The right to strike was made a contract right. The city dismissed the suit for fines. Muscare was released on March 13.

Labor unions gave little support to the strike. Bill Lee, President of the CFL, gave lukewarm support. Bob Gibson, President of the state AFL-CIO did not give any support. When the fire fighters union picketed McCormick Place the Teamsters sent goon squads armed with sticks. The fire fighters went to their car trunks and got axe handles. The Teamsters were repulsed.

There were four groups of firemen during the strike. These were the strikebreakers, the cadets, those who went back in, and those who stayed out. The city hired 700 strikebreakers during the 23 day strike. They had little or no training. The city would march these men in and out of fire houses for the media. After the strike a number of the 700 were fired. Many had police records or were wanted on warrants or indictments. Some firemen who went back in had Chicago residency problems and were going to be terminated sooner or later. The union did not encourage cadets in training to leave the fire houses. Union leaders did not think the strike would last longer than 72 hours and the union could not protect the trainees. As the strike progressed the union called for the cadets to leave. Many had relatives striking and did come out. None were fired. There were a total of 175 trained firemen who worked during the strike. Those firemen who stayed out are known in the fire houses as the 'Brothers of the Barrel'. This slogan arose when the strikers were picketing outside of fire houses during a cold February and were trying to keep warm with fires in 55 gallon drums. Some fire fighters contructed shacks outside their stations. After the strike patches were made up for those who struck. It became very bitter in the fire houses between those who struck and those who did not. To this day some members of the Department do not speak to one another.

In the aftermath of the strike there were significant changes. Frank Muscare was defeated in the next union election. Alderman Ed Burke said he was the "Winston Churchill of fire fighters." During the strike 24 Chicagoans died in fires in the 23 day period. In response the state legislature passed a law requiring compulsory arbitration and banning strikes for emergency workers (see Appendix B-6). As a result of the strike members of the union became very active in aldermanic and state elections. Judge Hechinger retired in 1986 when his name surfaced in the Operation Greylord investigation.

FIRST CHICAGO POLICE CONTRACT (1981)

The Chicago police were one of the last public sector groups to be organized. Part of the reason was that often the police found themselves in the position of being used as defenders of management during labor confrontations. In spite of this many labor organizations were working to organize the 12,000 member Chicago Police Department.

The Fraternal Order of Police had been lobbying the Illinois legislature since 1965 to generate a collective bargaining law for police. This had not met with success. In the aftermath of the fire fighters strike Mayor Byrne decided she would try to head off a similar debacle with the police. In the summer of 1980 Byrne said she wanted to know if the city's police officers wanted a single representative organization. In August, the mechanism was put in motion to have an election. Originally there were five organizations in the race to represent Chicago police officers. In addition to the FOP there was the Teamsters; the Confederation of Police (COP), associated with the AFL-CIO; Paperworkers Local 1975, also associated with the AFL-CIO; and the Chicago Patrolmen's Association. Another ballot alternative was city hall's position of "No Representation."

The organizations agreed among themselves and the city that to get ballot position each would have to show 1000 signatures in petitioned support of their organization. The winner of the first ballot and the runner-up would battle on a second ballot to be the winning representative. The first election was to be held October 16, 1980. Prior to that election, each organization was allowed to attend roll calls at various police

Police hold commemoration at site of Haymarket bomb (1969). This monument of fallen policeman was vandalized in the early 1970s and was placed in the Polic Academy.

facilities throughout the city. Representatives of each organization were allowed to address the police officers and explain their philosophy and record. John Dineen, FOP President during this time, feels the FOP won the election during these roll calls. The FOP representatives stressed they were the only group which had written a contract for police in Illinois. The FOP already had 70 contracts and recognitions of agreement signed in the state. Speakers for the FOP also told officers they were in favor of a no-strike clause as long as there was a mechanism for dispute resolution such as binding arbitration. FOP teams which hit the roll calls were instructed to wear ties and jackets. Some of the other groups tried to espouse the image of a Teamster. This did not go over too well with officers who thought of themselves as professionals. Mayor Byrne hurt the cause of City Hall when she announced the formation of a police brutality investigation committee. Police officers through out the city knew this had the potential of a 'kangaroo court' and because of the potential of misuse some sort of representation was needed.

The October 16 election was held on a payday and everyone who was on or off duty had a reason to come into the station. Over 9300 officers voted out of a total of 10,200 eligible. The city's position of 'No Representation' received 2471 votes. The FOP received 2050 votes; the Teamsters got 1876; the Paperworkers union carried 1591; the Confederation of Police got 927; and the Patrolmen's Association received 427 votes. This meant the FOP and No Representation would go head to head in the next round.

The city set the election for November 10 which was a Monday before a holiday. They were attempting to keep the vote down in hopes of defeating the FOP. The FOP knew that about 75 percent of the officers had voted for some sort of representation and they had to try to get those votes unified behind their union. FOP teams went back to the districts to argue for their positions. The FOP knew that if they won the election 51 percent to 49 percent they would have a weak bargaining position with the city. Most of the organizations who had lost the run-off either were neutral in the last election or opposed the FOP. Two days before the election Byrne announced police officers would get a six percent raise while the Superintendent was getting 86 percent. That did not go over well with the police. A total of 8995 policemen voted in the election. The FOP received almost 7400 votes or 82 percent.

With the victory the Chicago FOP, Lodge 7, became the largest single bargaining unit in the Fraternal Order of Police and the second largest bargaining unit in the nation. The Teamsters had a national plan to move into police ranks and that was largely defeated with the FOP victory in Chicago. The AFL-CIO police organization was also defeated. It was clear that police officers prefer organizations created by, for, and of their own. Victories in Chicago by both Fire Fighters Local 2 and Fraternal Order of Police Lodge 7 led to the public sector bargaining unit law in Illinois. This has spurred union bargaining victories in cities all over the state.

LIST OF IMPORTANT ABBREVIATIONS USED

AAISTW	AMALGAMATED ASSOCIATION of IRON, STEEL, and TIN WORKERS
AFL	AMERICAN FEDERATION OF LABOR
AMCBW	AMALGAMATED MEAT CUTTERS and BUTCHER WORKMEN
ARU	AMERICAN RAILWAY UNION
CFL	CHICAGO FEDERATION of LABOR
CHS	CHICAGO HISTORICAL SOCIETY
CIO	CONGRESS of INDUSTRIAL ORGANIZATIONS
CTF	CHICAGO TEACHERS FEDERATION
CTU	CHICAGO TEACHERS UNION
FE	FARM EQUIPMENT WORKERS
FEWOC	FARM EQUIPMENT WORKERS ORGANIZING COMMITTEE
FOP	FRATERNAL ORDER of POLICE
IWW	INTERNATIONAL WORKERS of the WORLD
NCOISW	NATIONAL COMMITTEE for ORGANIZING the IRON and STEEL WORKERS
SWOC	STEEL WORKERS ORGANIZING COMMITTEE
UAW	UNITED AUTO WORKERS
UGW	UNITED GARMENT WORKERS
USWA	UNITED STEELWORKERS of AMERICA
WLB	WAR LABOR BOARD

APPENDIX A

HIGHLIGHTS OF CHICAGO LABOR BATTLES

1855	April 21: Beer Riot near City Hall.
1865	Iron Molders Union meet in Chicago. This was the largest meeting of one craft ever to gather up to that time.
1867	May 1: Eight Hour Day Street Fights.
1873	December 22: Marchers numbering 10,000 come to City Hall demanding relief from the Depression. First of the "Bread Riots".
1877	July 23 - 26: National Railroad strike. Dozens are killed and millions in property are destroyed in Chicago.
1879	April: Military groups and marchers with guns are outlawed by Illinois legislature.
1885	June 30: Beginning of the Streetcar strike where workers are killed.
1886	May 1 - 2: Thousands march in Chicago calling for establishment of an eight hour day. This date was set in 1884 by the American Federation of Labor meeting in Chicago.
	May 3: One striker killed at the McCormick Reaper plant. Rally called for the next day at Haymarket Square.
	May 4: Bomb thrown during Haymarket rally and eight policemen are killed and many others injured.
	August 20: Eight convicted of conspiracy for Haymarket riot. Seven are sentenced to hang.
1887	October: Ft. Sheridan established as a means to keep order in Chicago.
	November 10 - 11: Five of Haymarket defendants die; four hang and one dies a suicide.
1889	Hull House opens.
1894	May 11 to July 20: Pullman strike. Union defeated through the use of injunctions and federal troops.
1896	July: William Jennings Bryan "Cross of Gold" speech at the Democratic Convention in Chicago.
1902	July 7 - 16: Teamster strike.

1903	June 5 - 19: Waiter's strike in the Loop.
	November 12 - 25: Streetcar strike.
1904	July: Meatpackers strike
1905	April 6 - July 20: Teamster strike, 25 die.
	June 27: Industrial Workers of the World (IWW) is formed at Chicago meeting.
	Upton Sinclair writes *The Jungle* exposing conditions in the meatpacking industry.
1910	September 22 - January 14, 1911: Garment workers strike which led to the founding of the Amalgamated Clothing workers.
1914	February to May 14: The Henrici strikes which clarify Illinois Boycott law.
1915	September 28 to December 23: Garment workers strike.
1919	July 30: Race riot which kills 38 and leaves 1000 homeless. September 21: Strike at steelmills begins.
1921	December: Meatpacking Union strikes Packinghouses to defend gains.
1937	May 30: Memorial Day Massacre at Republic Steel on South side. Ten die.
1944	April 12: Montgomery Ward's property seized by government after dispute with union.
1952	August 21: Strike by radical UE-FE against International Harvester.
1967	First Chicago Teachers Union contract.
1969	May 22: First Chicago Teachers Union strike.
1980	February: Chicago Firefighters Union strike.
1981	First contract signed with Chicago Fraternal Order of Police.
1985	July: Strike against the *Chicago Tribune* begins.

APPENDIX B - 1

THE EIGHT HOUR DAY BILL

This was the first eight hour day law. In 1867, when workers attempted to enforce the law with marches, street battles occurred in Chicago.

Eight Hour Bill

SECTION 1. On and after the first day of May, 1867, eight hours of labor, between the rising and the setting of the sum, in all mechanical trades, arts and employments and other cases of labor and service by the day, except in farm employments, shall constitute and be a legal day's work, where there is no special contract of agreement to the contrary.

SECTION 2. The act shall not apply to or in any way affect labor or service by the year, month or week, nor shall any person be prevented by anything herein contained from working as many hours overtime, or extra hours, as he or she may agree, and shall not, in any sense, be held to apply to farm labor.

SECTION 3. Repeals all acts inconsistent with this.

January 31, 1867 Springfield, Illinois

APPENDIX B - 2

GUN CONTROL IN THE LATE 1800s

Following the "bread riots" of the early 1870s, and other organized activities involving the foreign born, laws were passed to try and take guns from the people. Reprinted is the law establishing what became the Illinois National Guard. This made worker militia groups illegal in 1879.

The Military Code of Illinois

ARTICLE I

LIABILITY AND EXEMPTION

SECTION 1. Be it enacted ... That all able-bodied male citizens of this State between the ages of 18 and 45 years, ..., shall be subject to military duty and designated as the Illinois State Militia.

ARTICLE XI

GENERAL PROVISIONS.

SECTION 5. It shall not be lawful for any body of men whatever, other than the regular organized volunteer militia of this State, and the troops of the United States, to associate themselves together as a military company or organization, or to drill or parade with arms in any city or town of this state, without the license of the Governor thereof, which license may at any time be revoked.

SECTION 6. Whoever offends against the provisions of the proceeding section, or belongs to or parades with any such unauthorized body of men with arms, shall be punished by a fine not exceeding the sum of $10 or by imprisonment in the common jail for a term not exceeding six months, or both.

April 9, 1879 Springfield, Illinois

APPENDIX B - 3

THE CROSS OF GOLD SPEECH

The following is the text of the speech by William Jennings Bryan which he gave at the 1896 Democratic Convention in Chicago. The speech was part of the reform reaction to the defeat of labor in the 1894 Pullman strike. The speech is thought to have caused the nomination Bryan for President of the United States - an event which was unexpected by the public.

I would be presumptuous, indeed, to present myself against the distinguished gentlemen to who you have listened if this were a mere measuring of abilities; but this is not a contest between persons. The humblest citizen in all the land, when clad in the armor of a righteous cause, is stronger than all the hosts of error. I come to speak to you in defense of a cause as holy as the cause of liberty - the cause of humanity.

When this debate is concluded, a motion will be made to lay upon the table the resolution offered in commendation of the administration, and also the resolution offered in condemnation of the administration. We object to bringing this question down to the level of persons. The individual is but an atom; he is born, he acts, he dies; but principles are eternal; and this has been a contest over principle.

Never before in the history of this country has there been witnessed such a contest as that through which we have just passed. Never before in the history of American politics has a great issue been fought out as this issue has been, by the voters of a great party. On the fourth of March, 1895, a few Democrats, most of them members of Congress, issue an address to the Democrats of the nation, asserting that the money question was the paramount question of the hour; declaring that a majority of the Democratic party had the right to control the action of the party on this paramount issue; and concluding with the request that the believers in the free coinage of silver in the Democratic party should organize, take charge of, and control the policy of the Democratic party. Three months later, at Memphis, an organization was perfected, and the silver Democrats went forth openly and courageously proclaiming their belief, and declaring that, if successful, they would crystallize into a platform the declaration which they had made. Then began the conflict. With a zeal which inspired the crusaders who followed Peter the Hermit, our silver Democrats went forth from victory unto victory until they are now assembled, not to discuss, not to debate, but to enter up the judgment already rendered by the plain people of this country. In this contest brother has been arrayed against brother, father against son. The warmest ties of love, acquaintance and association has been disregarded; old leaders have been cast aside when they have refused to give expression to the sentiments of those they would lead, and new leaders have sprung up to give direction to this cause of truth. Thus has the contest been waged, and we have assembled here under as binding and solemn instructions were ever imposed upon representatives of the people.

We do not come as individuals. As individuals we might have been glad to compliment the gentleman from New York [Senator Hill], but we know that the people for whom we speak would never be willing to put him in a position where he could thwart the will of the Democratic party. I say it was not a question of persons; it was a question of principle, and it is not with gladness, my friends, that we find ourselves brought into conflict with those who are now arrayed on the other side.

The gentleman who preceded me [ex-Governor Russell] spoke of the State of Massachusetts; let me assure him that not one present in all this convention entertains the least hostility to the people of the State of Massachusetts, but we stand here representing people who are equals, before the law, of the greatest citizens in the State of Massachusetts. When you [turning to the gold delegates] come before us and tell us that we are about to disturb your business interests, we reply that you have disturbed our business interests by your course.

We say to you that you have made the definition of a businessman too limited in its application. The man who is employed for wages is as much a businessman as his employer, the attorney in a country town is as much a businessman as the corporation counsel in a great metropolis; the merchant at the crossroads store is as much a businessman as the merchant of New York; the farmer who goes forth in the morning and toils all day - who begins in the spring and toils all summer - and who by the application of brain and muscle to the natural resources of the country creates wealth, is as much a businessman as the man who goes upon the board of trade and bets upon the price of grain; the miners who go down a thousand feet into the earth, or climb two thousand feet upon the cliffs, and bring forth from their hiding places the precious metals to be poured into the channels of trade are as much businessmen as the few financial magnates who, in a back room, corner the money of the world. We come to speak for this broader class of businessmen.

Ah, my friends, we say not one word against those who live upon the Atlantic coast, but the hardy pioneers who have braved all the dangers of the wilderness, who have made the desert bloom as the rose - the pioneers away out there [pointing to the West], who rear their children near to Nature's heart, where they can mingle their voices with voices of the birds - out there where they have erected schoolhouses for the education of their young, churches where they praise their Creator, and cemeteries where rest the ashes of their dead - these people, we say, are as deserving of the consideration of our party as any people in the country. It is for these that we speak. We do not come as aggressors. Our war is not a war of conquest; we are fighting in the defense of our homes, our families, and posterity. We have petitioned, and our petitions have been scorned; we have entreated, and our entreaties have been disregarded; we have begged, and they have mocked when our calamity came. We beg no longer; we entreat no more; we petition no more. We defy them.

The gentleman from Wisconsin has said that he fears a Robespierre. My friends, in this land of the free you need not fear that a tyrant will spring up from among the people. What we need is an Andrew Jackson to stand, as Jackson stood, against the encroachments of organized wealth.

They tell as that this platform was made to catch votes. We reply to them that changing conditions made new issues; that the principles upon which the Democracy rests are as everlasting as the hills, but that they must be applied to new conditions as they arise. Conditions have arisen, and we are here to meet these conditions. They tell us that the income tax ought not to be brought in here; that it is a new idea. They criticize us for our criticism of the Supreme Court of the United States. My friends, we have not criticized; we have simply called attention to what you already know. If you want criticisms, read the dissenting opinions of the court. There you will find criticisms. They say that we passed an unconstitutional law; we deny it. The income-tax law was not unconstitutional when it was passed; it was not unconstitutional when it went before the Supreme Court for the first time; it did not become unconstitutional until one of the judges changed his mind, and we cannot be expected to know when a judge will change his mind. The income tax is just. It simply intends to put the burdens of government justly on the backs of the people. I am in favor of an income tax. When I find a man who is not willing to bear his share of the burdens of the government which protects him, I find a man who is unworthy to enjoy the blessings of a government like ours.

They say we are opposing national bank currency; it is true. If you will read what Thomas Benton said, you will find he said that, in searching history, he could find but one parallel to Andrew Jackson; that was Cicero, who destroyed the conspiracy of Cataline and saved Rome. Benton said that Cicero only did for Rome what Jackson did for us when he destroyed the bank conspiracy and saved America. We say in our platform that we believe that the right to coin and issue money is a function of government. We believe it. We believe that it is a part of sovereignty, and can no more with safety be delegated to private individuals than we could afford to delegate to private individuals the power to make penal statutes or levy taxes. Mr. Jefferson, who was once regarded as good Democratic authority, seems to have differed in opinion from the gentleman who has addressed us on the part of the minority. Those who are opposed to this proposition tell us that the issue of paper money is a function of the bank, and that the Government ought to go out of the banking business. I stand with Jefferson rather than with them, and tell them, as he did, that the issue of money is a function of government, and that the banks ought to go out of the governing business.

They complain about the plank which declares against life tenure in office. They have tried to strain it to mean that which it does not mean. What we oppose by that plank is the life tenure which is being built up in Washington, and which excludes from participation in official benefits the humbler members of society.

Let me call your attention to two or three important things. The gentleman from New York says that he will propose an amendment to the platform providing that the proposed change in our monetary system shall not affect contracts already made. Let me remind you that there is no intention of affecting those contracts which according to present laws are made payable in gold; but if he means to say that we cannot change our monetary system without protecting those who have loaned money before the change was made, I desire to ask him where, in law or in morals, he can find justification for not protecting the debtors when the act of 1873 was passed, if he now insists that we must protect the creditors.

He says he will also propose an amendment which will provide for the suspension of free coinage if we fail to maintain the parity within a year. We reply that when we advocate a policy which we believe will be successful, we are not compelled to raise a doubt as to our own sincerity by suggesting what we shall do if we fail. I ask him, if he would apply his logic to us, why he does not apply it to himself. He says he wants this country to try to secure an international agreement. Why does he not tell us what he is going to do if he fails to secure an international agreement? There is more reason for him to do that than there is for us to provide against the failure to maintain the parity. Our opponents have tried for twenty years to secure an international agreement, and those are waiting for it most patiently who do not want it at all.

And now, my friends, let me come to the paramount issue. If they ask us why it is that we say more on the money question than we say on the tariff question, I reply that, if protection has slain its thousands, the gold standard has slain its tens of thousands. If they ask us why we do not embody in our platform all the things we believe in, we reply that when we have restored the money of the Constitution all other necessary reforms will be possible; but that until this is done there is no other reform that can be accomplished.

Why is it that within three months such a change has come over the country? Three months ago, when it was confidently asserted that those who believe in the gold standard would frame our platform and nominate our candidates, even the advocates of the gold standard did not think that we could elect a President. And they had good reason for their doubt, because there is scarcely a state here today asking for the gold standard which is not in the absolute control of the Republican party. But note the change.

Mr. McKinley was nominated at St. Louis upon a platform which declared for the maintenance of the gold standard until it can be changed into bimetallism by international agreement. Mr. McKinley was the most popular man among the Republicans, and three months ago everybody in the Republican party prophesied his election. How is it today? Why, the man who was once pleased to think he looked like Napoleon - that man shudders today when he remembers that he was nominated on the anniversary of the battle of Waterloo. Not only that, but as he listens he can hear with ever-increasing distinctness the sound of waves as they beat upon the lonely shores of St. Helena.

Why this change? Ah, my friends, is not the reason for the change evident to any one who will look at the matter? No private character, however pure, no personal popularity, however great, can protect from the avenging wrath of an indignant people a man who will declare that he is in favor of fastening the gold standard upon this country, or who is willing to surrender the right of self-government and place the legislative control of our affairs in the hands of foreign potentates and powers.

We go forth confident that we shall win. Why? Because upon the paramount issue of this campaign there is not a spot of ground upon the enemy will dare to challenge battle. If they tell us that the gold standard is a good thing, we shall point to their platform and tell them that their platforms pledges the party to get rid of the gold standard and substitute bimetallism. If the gold standard is a good thing, why try to get rid of it? I call your attention to the fact that some of the very people who are in this convention today and who tell us that we ought to declare in favor of international bimetallism thereby declaring that the gold standard is wrong and that the principle of bimetallism is better - these very people four months ago were open and avowed advocates of the gold standard, and were then telling us that we could not legislate two metals together, even with the aid of all the world. If the gold standard is a good thing, we ought to declare in favor of its retention and not in favor of abandoning it; and if the gold standard is a bad thing why should we wait until the other nations are willing to help us to let go? Here is the line of battle, and we care not upon which issue they force the fight; we are prepared to meet them on either issue or on both. If they tell that the gold standard is the standard of civilization, we reply to them that this, the most enlightened of all the nations of the earth, has never declared for the gold standard and that both the great parties this year are declaring against it. If the gold standard is the standard of civilization, why, my friends, should we not have it? If they come to meet us on that issue we can present the history of our nation. More than that; we can tell them that they will search the pages of history in vain to find a single instance where the common people of any land have ever declared themselves in favor of the gold standard. They can find where the holders of fixed investments have declared for a gold standard, but not where the masses have.

Mr. Carlisle said in 1878 that this was a struggle between "the idle holders of idle capital" and "the struggling masses, who produce the wealth and pay the taxes of the country"; and, my friends, the question we are to decide is: Upon which side will the Democratic party fight; upon the side of "the idle holders of idle capital" or upon the side of "the struggling masses"? That is the question the party must answer first, and then it must be answered by each individual hereafter. The sympathies of the Democratic party, as shown by the platform, are on the side of the struggling masses who have ever been the foundation of the Democratic party. There are two ideas of government. There are those who believe that, if you will only legislate to make the well-to-do prosperous, their prosperity will leak through on those below. The Democratic idea, however, has been that if you legislate to make the masses prosperous, their prosperity will find its way up through ever class which rests upon them.

You come to us and tell us the great cities are in favor of the gold standard; we reply that the great cities rest upon our broad and fertile prairies. Burn down your cities and leave our farms, and your cities will spring up again as if by magic; but destroy our farms and the grass will grow in the streets of every city in the country.

My friends, we declare that this nation is able to legislate for its own people on every question, without waiting for the aid or consent of any other nation on earth; and upon that issue we expect to carry every state in the Union. I shall not slander the inhabitants of the fair State of Massachusetts nor the inhabitants of the State of New York by saying that, when they are confronted with the proposition, they will declare that this nation is not able to attend to its own business. It is the issue of 1776 over again. Our ancestors, when but three millions in number, had the courage to declare their political independence of every other nation; shall we, their descendants, when we have grown to seventy millions, declare that we are less independent that our forefathers? No, my friends, that will never be the verdict of our people. Therefore, we care not upon what lines the battle is fought. If they say bimetallism is good, but that we cannot have it until other nations help us, we reply that, instead of having a gold standard because England has, we will restore bimetallism, and let England have bimetallism because the United States has it. If they dare to come out in the open field and defend the gold standard as a good thing, we will fight them to the uttermost. Having behind us the producing masses of this nation and the world, supported by the commercial interests, the laboring interests, and the toilers everywhere, we will answer their demand for a gold standard by saying to them: You shall not press down upon the brow of labor this crown of thorns, you shall not crucify mankind upon a cross of gold.

APPENDIX B - 4

EARLY ATTEMPTS TO ORGANIZE IN THE PUBLIC SECTOR

The following is an article, by Margaret A. Haley, a Chicago teacher who was a founder of the American Federation of Teachers in 1916. She was an early teacher organizer and a founder of what eventually became the Chicago Teachers Union.

WHY TEACHERS SHOULD ORGANIZE

The responsibility for changing existing conditions so as to make it possible for the public school to do its work rests with the people, the whole people. Any attempt on the part of the public to evade or shift this responsibility must result in weakening the public sense of civic responsibility and the capacity for civic duty, besides further isolating the public school from the people, to the detriment of both.

The sense of responsibility for the duties of citizenship in a democracy is necessarily weak in a people so lately freed from monarchical rule as are the American people, and who still retain in their educational, economic, and political systems so much of their monarchical inheritance, with growing tendencies for retaining and developing the essential weakness of that inheritance instead of overcoming them.

Practical experience in meeting the responsibilities of citizenship directly, not in evading or shifting them, is the prime need of the American people. However clever or cleverly disguised the schemes for relieving the public of these responsibilities by vicarious performance of them, or however appropriate those schemes in a monarchy, they have no place in a government of the people, by the people, and for the people, and such schemes must result in defeating their object; for to the extent that they obtain they destroy in a people the capacity for self-government.

If the American people cannot be made to realize and meet their responsibility to the public school, no self-appointed custodians of the public intelligence and conscience can do it for them. Horace Mann, speaking of the dependence of the prosperity of the schools on the public intelligence, said:

The people will sustain no better schools and have no better education than they personally see the need of; and therefore the people are to be informed and elevated as a preliminary step toward elevating the schools.

Sometimes, in our impatience at the slowness with which the public moves in these matters, we are tempted to disregard this wise counsel.

The methods as well as the objects of teachers' organizations must be in harmony with the fundamental object of the public school in a democracy, to preserve and develop the democratic ideal. It is not enough that this ideal be realized in the administration of the schools and the methods of teaching; in all its relations to the public, the public school must conform to this ideal.

The character of teachers' organizations is twofold. Organizations on professional lines existed before the necessity became apparent for those for the improvement of conditions. The necessity for both is becoming increasingly evident, and the success of the one is dependent upon the success of the other. Unless the conditions for realizing educational ideals keep pace with the ideals themselves, the result in educational practice is deterioration. To know the better way and be unable to follow it is unfavorable to a health development. To have freedom in the conditions without the incentive of the ideal is no less harmful. It is, therefore, opportune that the occasion for the organization in the newer sense, the sense understood in the subject of this paper, should be coincident with the formulation of the most advanced educational theory in a practical philosophy of pedagogy.

Modern education thought has been dominated by the element of inspiration and the element of science; the former enthroning the child, displacing the subject-matter of knowledge as the center of educational theory; the latter founded upon the faith in underlying laws of human development in harmony with which it is possible to evolve a rational method of eliminating waste in the educational process.

How far the educational influence of teaching under these two motives tends to produce a teaching body capable of the highest kind of organized activity it is not possible to determine. Neither it is possible not to perceive the harmony between the principles underlying a rational system of teaching and those underlying the movement for freer expression and better conditions among teachers.

There is no possible conflict between the interest of the child an the interest of the teacher, and nothing so tends to make this fact evident as the progress in the scientific conception of educational method and administration. For both the child and the teacher freedom is the condition of development. The atmosphere in which it is easiest to teach is the atmosphere in which it is easiest to learn. The same things that are a burden to the teacher are a burden also to the child. The same things which restrict her powers restrict his powers also.

The element of danger in organization for self-protection is the predominance of the selfish motive. In the case of teachers a natural check is placed on this motive by the necessity for professional organization. The closer the union between these two kinds of organization, the fuller and more effective is the activity possible to each.

Freedom of activity directed by freed intelligence is the ideal of democracy. This ideal of democracy is slowly shaping our educational ideal, and making its realization the function of our educational agencies.

The public school is the organized means provided by the deliberate effort of the whole people to free intelligence at its source - and thru freed intelligence to secure freedom of action.

Misdirected activity is proof that the educational agencies are not properly functioning. This may be because these agencies have not freed intelligence, or it may be because the intelligence which they have freed is denied free activity.

Misdirected political activity in lowering the democratic ideal, reacts to lower the educational ideal. On the other hand, a false or incomplete educational ideal fails to free the intelligence necessary for the work of constructing a democracy out of our monarchial inheritance.

That the public school does not fell its responsibility in the matter of political corruption, for instance, nor realize the effect upon the schools of this corruption and the misdirected activity of which it is a symptom, is proof that the public school is not yet conscious of its own vital function in a democracy.

When Ida Tarbell and Lincoln Steffens in lightening flashes, disclosed to the American people indisputable facts concerning the business methods of our so-called "good business men" and their relations to politics, they showed a condition of affairs that must make every thoughtful citizen stop and ask: "Whither are we going?" How many public-school teachers, on reading these disclosures, said to themselves: "We must take our share of the blame. The public school, that great agency of the people for freeing intelligence, has failed to do its whole duty." The public school is not wholly to blame. There are other educational agencies. There is the press, for instance. But the press does not belong to the people; it is a private enterprise. The schools do belong to the people, and they are free.

We teachers are responsible for existing conditions to the extent that the schools have not inspired true ideals of democracy, or that we have not made the necessary effort toward removing the conditions which make the realization of these ideals impossible.

We recognize anarchy in the act which takes the life of the chief executive of a city, state, or nation; but there is another kind of anarchy in our midst. It is the anarchy which sends the railroad and corporations lobby to the legislatures and to the taxing bodies - yes, even to the bench - and in whose hands these servants of the people are as wax and obey the command of the lobby, and defy the law they were elected and sworn to uphold. This is the anarchy we need to fear in America, and whose meaning the public-school teachers need to comprehend.

It was indeed an invaluable public service which the teachers of Chicago rendered when they established in the courts, and in the minds of the people, the fact that thru the connivance of public officials five public-utility corporations are enabled to rob Chicago of ten million dollars annually thru the free gift to these corporations of the use of the public streets. Think what that means: the second city in the Union compelled to pay to five corporations, her own creatures, an annual tribute of ten million dollars; more than the combined cost of maintaining the public schools and the public library - at the same time her board of education closing the schools, cutting the teachers' salaries, increasing the number of children in each room, and otherwise crippling the service for want of money!

America's motto once was, "Millions for defense, but not one cent for tribute," and we teachers may continue to teach that it is still our motto; but the children will learn, in spite of our teaching, that "Millions for tribute and not one cent for defense" is nearer to the truth.

The significant thing in the tax crusade of the Chicago teachers was not the disclosing of these humiliating facts, nor the forcing of the corporations to return to the public treasury some of their stolen million; it was that the public school, thru the organized effort of the teachers, was the agency which brought these conditions to the attention of the public and showed how to apply the remedy.

Nowhere in the United States today does the public school, as a branch of the public service, receive from the public either the moral or financial support needed to enable it properly to perform its important function in the social organism. The conditions which are militating most strongly against efficient teaching, and which existing organizations of the kind under discussion here are directing their energies toward changing, briefly stated are the following:

1. Greatly increased cost of living, together with constant demands for higher standards of scholarship and professional attainments and culture, to be met with practically stationary and wholly inadequate teacher' salaries.
2. Insecurity of tenure of office and lack of provision for old age.
3. Overwork in overcrowded schoolrooms, exhausting both mind and body.
4. And lastly, lack of recognition of the teacher as an educator in the school system, due to the increased tendency toward "factoryizing education," making the teacher an automaton, a mere factory hand, whose duty it is to carry out mechanically and unquestioningly the ideas and orders of those clothed with the authority of position, and who may or may not know the needs of the children or how to minister to them.

The individuality of the teacher and her power of initiative are thus destroyed, and the result is courses of study, regulations, and equipment which the teacher had no voice in selecting, which often have no relation to the childrens' needs, and which prove a hindrance instead of a help in teaching.

Dr. John Dewey, of the University of Chicago, in the *Elementary School Teacher* for December, 1903, says:

As to the teacher: If there is a single public-school system in the United States where there is official and constitutional provision made for submitting questions of methods of discipline and teaching, and the questions of the curriculum, text-books, etc., to the discussion of those actually engaged in the work of teaching, that fact has escaped my notice. Indeed, the opposite situation is so common that it seems, as a rule, to be absolutely taken for granted as the normal and final condition of affairs. The number of persons to whom any other course has occurred as desirable, or even possible - to say nothing of necessary - if apparently very limited. But until the public-school system is organized in such a way that every teacher has some regular and representative way in which he or she can register judgment upon matters of educational importance, with the assurance that this judgment will somehow affect the school system, the assertion that the present system is not, from the internal standpoint, democratic seems to be justified. Either we come here upon some fixed and inherent limitation of the democratic principle, or else we find in this fact an obvious discrepancy so great as to demand immediate and persistent effort at reform.

A few days ago Professor George F. James, dean of pedagogy of the State University of Minnesota, said to an audience of St. Paul teachers:

One hundred thousand teachers will this year quit an occupation which does not yield them a living wage. Scores and hundreds of schools are this day closed in the most prosperous sections of this country because the bare pittance offered will not attract teachers of any kind.

Professor James further maintained that school-teachers are not only underpaid, but that they are paid much less proportionately than they received eight years ago.

It is necessary that the public understand the effect which teaching under these conditions is having on the education of the children.

In reacting unfavorably upon the public school, these wrong conditions affect the child, the parent, and the teacher; but the teacher is so placed that she is the one first to feel the disadvantage: she is held responsible by the child, by the parent, by the authorities, by society, and by herself because of her own ideals, for duties in the performance of which she is continually hampered. The dissatisfaction and restlessness among teachers are due to the growing consciousness that causes outside of themselves and beyond their control are making their work more difficult. Some of these causes of irritation are inherent in the school system. Such proceed from the failure of the system on the educational and administrative side to adapt itself to the growing ideals of education and the demand for rational methods of realizing them. These inherent causes of trouble include the limitations of the teachers themselves and the failure of the system either to remedy these deficiencies or to remove the deficient.

Where friction is minimized by enlightened supervision and administration, the pressure of outside causes is less keenly felt. But where the system is so administered that inherent weaknesses and outside causes combine and reinforce each other to produce dissatisfaction, the double pressure increases the irritation, and correspondingly hastens the time when sheer necessity impels the teachers to seek a remedy or leave the profession.

The first and crudest form of expression that dissatisfaction with these conditions takes is the reaction against the nearest and most obvious form of irritation - unsatisfactory supervision and administration, which are later recognized as effects rather than causes. The last causes to be assigned are the real ones, and only when every individual effort to better conditions has failed does the thought of combined effort for mutual aid - in other words, organized effort - suggest itself.

And yet organization is the method of all intelligently directed effort.

Within the last decade in a few cities of the United States organization has been effected among those on whom devolves the responsibility of applying scientific principles to the actual work with children in the school-room, the purpose of such organization being to secure conditions under which rational teaching may become possible.

Such organization is at once the effect and the cause of a broadening of the intelligence and the educational outlook of the teachers, for to such organization they must take not only a reading acquaintance with the best in educational theory and practice, but a practical knowledge of what constitutes scientific teaching. Nor is this all, tho it may suffice for the professional equipment of those whose duties are merely supervisory. The class-room teachers in addition to this must have the ability and skill, given fair conditions, to do scientific teaching. More than this, they must know the conditions under which scientific teaching is possible, must know when and in what respects such conditions are lacking; and then, most difficult of all, because it includes all these and much more, they must know how to reach the public with accurate information concerning the conditions under which teaching is done and their effects on the work of the school.

Such are the prerequisites of teachers who would successfully engage in the work of securing better conditions for themselves, and for the schools, thru organization.

A word, before closing, on the relations of the public-school teachers and the public schools to the labor unions. As the professional organization furnishes the motive and ideal which shall determine the character and methods of the organized effort of teachers to secure better conditions for teaching, so is it the province of the educational agencies in a democracy to furnish the motive and ideal which shall determine the character and methods of the organization of its members for self-protection.

There is no possible conflict between the good of society and the good of its members, of which the industrial workers are the vast majority. The organization of these workers for mutual aid has shortened the hours of labor, raised and equalized the wages of men and women, and taken the children from the factories and workshops. These humanitarian achievements of the labor unions - and many others which space forbids enumerating - in raising the standard of living of the poorest and weakest members of society, are a service to society which for its own welfare it must recognize. More than this, by intelligent comprehension of the limitations of the labor unions and the causes of these limitations, by just, judicious, and helpful criticism and co-operation, society must aid them to feel the inspiration of higher ideals, and to find the better means to realize these ideals.

If there is one institution on which the responsibility to perform this service rests most heavily, it is the public school. If there is one body of public servants of whom the public has a right to expect the mental and moral equipment to face the labor question, and other issues vitally affecting the welfare of society and urgently pressing for a rational and scientific solution, it is the public-school teachers, whose special contribution to society is their own power to think, the moral courage to follow their convictions, and the training of citizens to think and to express thought in free and intelligent action.

The narrow conception of education which makes the mechanics of reading, writing, and arithmetic, and other subjects, the end and aim of the schools, instead of a means to an end - which mistakes the accidental and incidental for the essential - produces the unthinking, mechanical mind in teacher and pupil, and prevents the public school as an institution, and the public-school teachers as a body, from becoming conscious of their relation to society and its problems, and from meeting their responsibilities. On the other hand, that teaching which is most scientific and rational gives the highest degree of power to think and to select the most intelligent means of expressing thought in every field of activity. The ideals and methods of the labor unions are in a measure a test of the efficiency of the schools and other educational agencies.

How shall the public school and the industrial workers, in their struggle to secure the rights of humanity thru a more just and equitable distribution of the products of their labor, meet their mutual responsibility to each other and to society?

Whether the work of co-ordinating these two great educational agencies, manual and mental labor, with each other and with the social organism, shall be accomplished thru the affiliation of the organizations of brain and manual workers is a mere matter of detail and method to be decided by the exigencies in each case. The essential thing is that the public-school teachers recognize the fact that their struggle to maintain the efficiency of the schools thru better conditions for themselves is part of the same great struggle which the manual workers - often misunderstood and unaided - have been making for themselves and their children; and that lack of unfavorable conditions of both is a common cause.

Two ideals are struggling for supremacy in American life today: one the industrial ideal, culminating thru supremacy of commercialism, which subordinates the worker to the product and the machine; the other, the ideal of democracy, the ideal of the educators, which places humanity above all machines, and demands that all activity shall be the expression of life. If this ideal of the educators cannot be carried over into the industrial field, then the ideal of industrialism will be carried over into the school. Those two ideals can no more continue to exist in American like than our nation could have continued half slave and half free. If the school cannot bring joy to the work of the world, the joy must go out of its own life, and work in the school as in the factory will become drudgery.

Viewed in this light, the duty and responsibility of the educators in the solution of the industrial question is one which must thrill and fascinate while it awes, for the very depth of the significance of life is put up in this question. But the first requisite is to put aside all prejudice, all preconceived notions, all misinformation and half-information, and to take to this question what the educators have long recognized must be taken to scientific investigation in other fields. There may have been justification for failure to do this in the past, but we cannot face the responsibility of continued failure and maintain our title as thinkers and educators. When men organize and go out to kill, they go surrounded by pomp, display, and pageantry, under the inspiration of music and with the admiration of the throng. Not so the army of industrial toilers who have been fighting humanity's battles, unhonored and unsung.

It will be well indeed if the teachers have the courage of their convictions and face all that the labor unions have faced with the same courage and perseverance.

Today, teachers of America, we stand at the parting of the ways. Democracy is not on trial, but America is.

From: *Addresses and Proceedings of the National Education Association,*
43rd Annual Meeting, St. Louis, 1904 (Washington, D.C.: The Association, 1904), pp. 144-53

APPENDIX B - 5

DOCUMENTS FROM THE EFFORT TO ORGANIZE THE STEEL INDUSTRY

REPUBLIC STEEL'S STATEMENT CONCERNING THE STEEL WORKER ORGANIZING COMMITTEE

(This letter was sent by Republic Steel to all its employees in July, 1936.)

To Our Employees:

We are making the following statement so that you will know the attitude of Republic toward the recently announced campaign for unionization of the steel workers.

The leader of this drive is John L. Lewis, head of the Coal Miner's Union. He is not connected with the steel industry.... Representatives of radical and communist groups are helping in this movement. William Z. Foster, chairman of the Communist Party, has announced his support. Foster was the leader in the unsuccessful attempt to unionize the steel industry in 1919. What Do They Want? John L. Lewis and his organization want more workers to pay them dues .... If they could organize the steel workers they hope to collect $5,000,000 a year from them. Republic employees alone would pay over half a million dollars. Furthermore, they could place dues and assessments at any figure they liked and the steel workers would have to pay them.

The real aim of the present organization drive is to establish a closed shop. They want to force you into the union and make you pay for the right to work. Under a "Closed Shop" every man has to pay his dues to the union whether he wants to or not. If he gets behind in dues, they can throw him out of the union. By this threat they can keep the dues rolling in.

One of the announced purposes of this drive is to throw out your Employee Representation Plan whom you have elected for collective bargaining with the management. The union wants to destroy all Employee Representation Plans in the steel industry.

Your Employee Representation Plan is not run by outsiders. It works. Under your plan, you select your own Employee Representatives --men you know and with whom you work. Under a union you would represented by outsiders who may know little or nothing about your problems, your management, or the steel industry. Furthermore, you would have no choice in their selection. You would have to pay money to be dictated to by somebody you did not even know. What Are There Methods?

The methods customarily used by professional union agitators and organizers are force, coercion, and intimidation of workers and their families. They threaten to call a strike to force men to join their union. They try to force mills to stop operation and keep men from their work for months at a time. They do this to scare men into their union whom they know do not want to join the union. What is Republic's Stand?

Republic stands for the open shop principle.

No employee has to join any organization to get or hold a job. Advancement depends on individual merit and effort.

Republic will not permit any activities within its plant which will:
1. Interfere with the orderly conduct of its operations.
2. Stir up strife or discontent.
3. Threaten the peace and comfort of its workers and their families.

Every Republic employee owes a duty of loyalty to the Company so that its best interests may be served. Conduct detrimental to the interests of the Company and which may disrupt the satisfactory relations between employees and management will not be tolerated.

THE FIRST LABOR AGREEMENT IN THE STEEL INDUSTRY

Reprinted below is the first labor agreement between United States Steel, also known as Big Steel, and the Steelworkers Union. On Memorial Day, 1937, the marchers at Republic Steel, which was part of the Little Steel group, were attempting to get the same type of agreement at their plant.

AGREEMENT

This Agreement, dated March 17, 1937, between Carnegie-Illinois Steel Corporation (hereinafter referred to as the "Corporation") and the Steel Workers Organizing Committee on behalf of the members of the Amalgamated Association of Iron, Steel and Tin Workers of North America, or its successor, (hereinafter referred to as the "UNION") employed by the Corporation, made pursuant to and in supplement of Section 4 of the Agreement of March 2, 1937, between said parties.

Section 1. It is the intent and purpose of the parties hereto that this Agreement will promote and improve industrial and economic relationships between those employees who are members of the Union and the Corporation, and to set forth herein the basic Agreement covering rates of pay, hours of work and conditions of employment to be observed between the parties hereto.

It is understood and agreed that this Agreement pertains only to members of the Union employed in the corporation's steel manufacturing and by-product coke products.

The term "employee", as used in this Agreement, shall not include Foremen, Assistant Foremen or Supervisors in charge of any classes of labor, or Watchmen, or any salaried employees.

Section 2 - Recognition. The Corporation recognizes the Union as the collective bargaining agency for those employees of the Corporation who are members of the Union. The Corporation recognizes and will not interfere with the right of its employees to become members of the Union. There shall be no discrimination, interference, restraint or coercion by the Corporation or any of its agents against any members because of membership in the Union. The Union agrees not to intimidate or coerce employees into membership and also not to solicit membership on Corporation time or plant property.

Section 3 - Wages. Effective March 16, 1937, there shall be an increase in wages of ten cents (10¢) an hour on all rates which are at present Four Dollars and twenty cents ($4.20) a day, or a minimum for this classification of Five Dollars ($5.00) a day of eight (8) hours. Such classifications now receiving less than Four Dollars and twenty cents ($4.20) a day or less than fifty-two and one-half cents (52¢) per hour, shall be increased ten cents (10¢) per hour. There shall be an increase of ten cents (10¢) per hour in all other hourly rates, and an equivalent increase in all tonnage and piece-work rates (which will not under normal expected earning [an] increase) of not less than eighty cents (80¢) per day of eight (8) hours.

Section 4 - Hours of Work. Effective March 16, 1937, there shall be established an eight (8) hour day and a forty (40) hour week. Time and one-half shall be paid for all overtime in excess of eight (8) hours in any one day or for all overtime in excess of forty (40) hours in any one week.

A day may be a calendar day or any 24-hour period, and a week may be a calendar week or any five (5) regular 8-hour turns on consecutive days, followed by a 48-hour rest period, at the option of the Corporation.

An employee, who is a member of the Union, shall not be paid both daily and weekly overtime for the same hours do worked.

Section 5 - Vacations. Each employee, who is a member of the union and who (prior to July 1, 1937) was continually in the service of the Corporation five (5) years or more (continuity of service to be based on United States Steel and Carnegie Pension Fund Rules for Service continuity) shall receive one week's vacation with pay, such vacation to be taken in a single period. Those who are granted vacations will be paid on their average rate of earnings per hour for the two pay periods immediately preceding their vacation. The total hours of vacation pay will be the average hours they worked per week during that period, but not less than 40 hours nor more than 48 hours.

Vacations will, so far as possible, be granted at times most desired by employees, but the final right to allotment of vacation period is exclusively reserved to the Corporation in order to insure the orderly operation of the Plants.

Section 6 - Seniority. It is understood and agreed that in all cases of promotion and increase or decrease of forces the following factors shall be considered and where factors (b), (c), (d) and (e) are relatively equal, length of continuous service shall govern.

  (a) Length of continuous service.
  (b) Knowledge, training, ability, skill and efficiency.
  (c) Physical fitness.
  (d) Family status; number of dependents, etc.
  (e) Place of residence.

Section 7 - Adjustment of Grievances. Should differences arise between the corporation and the Union or its members employed by the Corporation as to the meaning and application of the provisions of this Agreement, or should any local trouble of any kind arise in any plant, there shall be no suspension of work on account of such differences, but an earnest effort shall be made to settle such differences immediately in the following matter:

* First, between the aggrieved employee, who is a member of the Union, and the Foreman of the department involved;

* Second, between a member or members of the Grievance Committee, designated by the Union, and the Foreman and Superintendent of Department;

* Third, between a member or members of the Grievance Committee, designated by the Union, and the General Superintendent or Manager of the Plant;

* Fourth, between the Representatives of the National organization of the Union and the Representatives of the Executives of the Corporation;

* Fifth, in the event the dispute shall not have been satisfactorily settled, the matter shall then be appealed to an impartial umpire to be appointed by mutual agreement of the parties hereto. The decision of the umpire shall be final. The expense and salary incident to the services of the umpire shall be paid jointly by the Corporation and the Union.

Specified periods shall be agreed upon between the Grievance Committee and the General Superintendent or Manage of each plant for the presentation of grievances hereunder; provided, however, that matters pertaining to discharge (or other matters that cannot reasonably be delayed until the time of the next regular meeting) may be presented at any time in accordance with the foregoing provisions.

The Grievance Committee for each plant shall consist of not less than three employees of that plant, and not more than ten (10) such employees, designated by the Union; who will be afforded such time off, without pay, as may be required:

* First, to attend regularly scheduled committee meetings,

* Second, to attend meeting pertaining to discharges or other matters which cannot be reasonably be delayed until the time of the next regular meeting, and

* Third, any member of the Grievance Committee shall have the right to visit departments other than his own at all reasonable times for the purpose of transacting the legitimate business of the Grievance Committee, after notice to and permission from his department superintendent or his designated representative.

The actual number of members of the Grievance Committee at each plant shall be mutually agreed upon between the General Superintendent or Manager of the plant and the Union, and in no case shall there be more than one member in any department.

Section 8 - Management. The management of the works and the direction of the working forces, including the right to hire, suspend or discharge for proper cause, or transfer, and the right to relive employees from duty because of lack of work, or for some legitimate reasons, is vested exclusively in the Corporation, provided that this will not be used for purposes of discrimination against any member of the Union.

Section 9 - Discharge Cases. In the event a member of the Union shall be discharged from his employment from and after the date hereof, and he believes he has been unjustly dealt with, such discharge shall constitute a case arising under the method of adjusting grievances herein provided. In the even it should be decided under the rules of this Agreement that an injustice has been dealt the employee with regard to the discharge, the Corporation shall reinstate such employee and pay full compensation at the employee's regular rate of pay for the time lost. All such cases of discharge shall be taken up and disposed of within five (5) days from the date of discharge.

Section 10 - Safety and Health. The Corporation shall continue to make reasonable provisions for the safety and health of its employees at the plant during the hours of their employment. Protective devices, wearing apparel and other equipment necessary to properly protect employees from injury shall be provided by the Corporation in accordance with practice now prevailing in each separate plant. Proper heating and ventilating systems shall be installed where needed.

Section 11 - Individual Wage Rates. Where alleged inequalities in wage rates prevail, the matter may be taken up for local plant adjustment and settlement made on a mutually satisfactory basis.

Section 12 - Future Conferences. Joint conferences between Representatives of the Corporation and of the Union shall commence in Pittsburgh, Pa., on February 7, 1938, for the purpose of negotiating an Agreement with regards to wages, hours and working conditions, to take effect upon the expiration of this Agreement.

Section 13 - Holidays. The following days shall be considered Holidays, during which says there shall be no regular production work, except in cases of continuous operations, on
> July 4th,
> Labor Day, and
> Christmas.

Section 14 - Termination Date. This Agreement shall remain in full force and effect until February 28, 1938 inclusive.

CARNEGIE - ILLINOIS STEEL CORPORATION   By B. F. Fairless, President
STEEL WORKERS ORGANIZING COMMITTEE   By Phillip Murray, Chairman

APPENDIX B - 6

THE ILLINOIS PUBLIC LABOR RELATIONS ACT

After the Chicago Fire fighters strike in 1980 the Illinois legislature was determined to prevent a repeat. They passed the Illinois Labor Relations Act which mandated binding arbitration for police and fire fighter disputes. This law became effective July 1, 1984. Relevant portions are printed below.

ACT 315. ILLINOIS PUBLIC LABOR RELATIONS ACT

Section 14. Security Employee, Peace Officer and Fire Fighter Disputes.

(a) In the case of collective bargaining agreements involving units of security employees of a public employer, Peace Officer Units, or units of fire fighters or paramedics, and in the case of disputes under Section 18 (*Ed. Note - Strikes presenting a clear and present danger to the public - DN*), unless the parties mutually agree to some other time limit, mediation shall commence 30 days prior to the expiration date of such agreement or at such later time as the mediation services chosen under subsection (b) of Section 12 can be provided to the parties.

(g) At or before the conclusion of the hearing held pursuant to subsection (d), the arbitration panel shall identify the economic issues in dispute, and direct each of the parties to submit, within such time limit as the panel shall prescribe, to the arbitration panel and to each other its last offer of settlement on each economic issue. The determination of the arbitration panel as to the issues in dispute and as to which of these issues are economic shall be conclusive. The arbitration panel, within 30 days after conclusion of the hearing, or such further additional periods to which the parties may agree, shall make written findings of fact and promulgate a written copy thereof to the parties and their representatives and to the Board. As to each economic issue, the arbitration panel shall adopt the last offer of settlement which, in the opinion of the arbitration panel, more nearly complies with the applicable factors prescribed in subsection (h). The findings, opinions and order as to all other issues shall be based upon the applicable factors prescribed in subsection (h).

(h) Where there is no agreement between the parties, or where there is an agreement but the parties have begun negotiations or discussions looking to a new agreement or amendment of the existing agreement, and wage rates or other conditions of employment under the proposed new or amended agreement are in dispute, the arbitration panel shall base its findings, opinions and order upon the following factors, as applicable:

(1) The lawful authority of the employer.
(2) Stipulations of the parties.
(3) The interests and welfare of the public and the financial ability of the unit of government to meet those costs.
(4) Comparison of the wages, hours ad conditions of employment of the employees involved in the arbitration proceeding with the wages, hours and conditions of employment of other employees performing similar services and with other employees generally:
(A) In public employment in comparable communities.

(B) In private employment in comparable communities.

(5) The average consumer prices for goods and services, commonly known as the cost of living.

(6) The overall compensation presently received by the employees, including direct wage compensation, vacations, holidays and other excused time, insurance and pensions, medical and hospitalization benefits, the continuity and stability of employment and all other benefits received.

(7) Changes in any of the foregoing circumstances during the pendency of the arbitration proceedings.

(8) Such other factors, not confined to the foregoing, which are normally or traditionally taken into consideration in the determination of wages, hours and conditions of employment through voluntary collective bargaining, mediation, fact-finding, arbitration or otherwise between the parties, in the public service or in private employment.

(k) Orders of the arbitration panel shall be reviewable, upon appropriate petition by either the public employer or the exclusive bargaining representative, by the circuit court for the county in which the dispute arose or in which a majority of affected employees reside, but only for reasons that the arbitration panel was without or exceeded its statutory authority; the order is arbitrary, or capricious; or the order was procured by fraud, collusion or other similar and unlawful means.

(m) Security officers of public employers, and Peace Officers, Fire Fighters and fire department and fire protection district paramedics, covered by this Section may not withhold services, nor may public employers lock out or prevent such employees from performing services at any time.

APPENDIX C

SELECTED SOURCES AND FURTHER READING

Primary Sources

Periodicals

The Chicago daily or weekly press includes the *Daily News, Democratic Press, Tribune, Times, American, Herald, Herald American, Sun-Times, Times and Evening Post.*

Other organization periodicals include:

The Alarm, edited by Albert Parsons and D.D. Lum (1884-1889);
The Alarm, edited by Lucy Parsons (1915-1916);
American Federationist;
Anarchist, edited by George Engel and Adolph Fisher (1886);
CIO News;
Harpers' Monthly Magazine;
Harpers' Weekly;
Leslie's Weekly; and
Steel Labor.

Government Documents And Other Primary Material

Fifth Annual Report of the Commissioner of Labor, 1889, *Railroad Labor*, 51st Congress., 1st Session, House of Rep., Doc. No. 336, 1890.
Report of the Senate Committee on Education and Labor, 76th Congress, 1st Session, *Labor Policies of Employer Organizations*, 1939.
U.S. Strike Commission, *Report of the Chicago Strike of June-July 1894*, 53rd Congress, 3rd Session, Senate Document No. 7, 1895.
Altgeld, J.P., *Reasons for Pardoning the Haymarket Anarchists* (1986).
Darrow, C., *The Story of My Life* (1932).
Gompers, S., *Seventy Years of Life and Labor* (1925).
Lloyd, H.D., *Wealth Against Commonwealth* (1902).
Martin, E.W., *The History of the Great Riots* (1877).
Olds, M., *Analysis of the Interchurch World Movement Report on the Steel Strike* (1922).
Sinclair, U., *The Jungle*, (1906).
Spies, A., *His Speech in Court and General Notes* (1887).

In addition there are several sources for historical collections. The Chicago Historical Society has the primary collection of photographs, letters, maps, leaflets, and records which relate to Chicago trade union strikes. There are vast material on other major demonstrations as well. The Illinois State Historical Society in Springfield contains collections relating to both Haymarket and Pullman. There are also copies of many of the Chicago workers' organization newspapers. The Illinois State Archives in Springfield contains many of the papers of Governors Oglesby and Altgeld as well as others.

Secondary Books and Articles

Adelman, W.J., *Haymarket Revisited* (1986).
Andreas, A.T., *History of Cook County* (1884).
Andrews, W., *Battle for Chicago* (1946).
Avrich, P., *The Haymarket Tragedy* (1984).
Boyer, R.O. and Morais, H.M., *Labor's Untold Story* (1955).
Brecher, J., *Strike!* (1972).
Chicago History, Quarterly of the Chicago Historical Society.
Chicagoland Chamber of Commerce, *Chicago: Center of Enterprise* (1982).
David, H., *The History of the Haymarket Affair* (1936).
Dedmon, E., *Fabulous Chicago: A Great City's History and People* (1983).
Dulles, F.R., *Labor in America: A History* (1966).
Farr, F., *Chicago* (1973).
Gutman, H.G. et al., *Who Built America?*, Volume One (1989).
Haley, M.A., *Battleground: The Autobiography of Margaret A. Haley* edited by Reid, R.L. (1982).
Labor's Heritage, Quarterly of the George Meany Memorial Archives (1989 -).
Sloan, A.A., *Hoffa* (1993).
Smith, C., *Urban Disorder and the Shape of Belief* (1995).

INDEX

Addams, Jane 48, 50
Altgeld, John Peter (Governor) 44, 46, 48, 52, 59

Beer Riots 15
Bonfield, (Captain) 31, 39, 44
Bread Riot 24
Bryan, Willaim Jennings 59
Byrne, Jane (Mayor) 128, 129, 131, 132, 133, 135

Daley, Richard J. (Mayor) 127, 128
Daley, Richard M. (State Senator) 131
Darrow, Clarence 44, 46, 69
Debs, Eugene 51, 52, 59
Dorfman, Allen 94
Dorfman, Paul 94

Farley, James 62, 69
Fielden, Samuel 39, 41, 44, 46
Fischer, Adolph 36, 39, 41, 44
Fort Sheridan 26, 46, 52
Foster, William Z. 86, 89

Gary, Joseph (Judge) 41, 44, 46
Girdler, Tom 95
Gompers, Samuel 44, 62
Great Lakes Naval Base 26, 46
Great Rail Strike of 1877 26, 59

Haley, Margaret 125
Hart, Schaffner & Marx 76
Haymarket 15, 31, 33, 46, 48, 59
Hillman, Sidney 77
Hoffa, Jimmy 94
Hoffman, F.A. 21
Hull-House 48, 50

Illinois National Guard 31
Industrial Workers of the World (IWW) 67, 68, 89

Jackson, Jesse 132

Kelly, Florence 48

Kennedy, Edward (Senator) 132
Kennedy, John F. (President) 94
Kennedy, Robert (Attorney General) 94
Knights of Labor 33, 36
Know Nothings 12, 13

Lewis, John L. 95

Marcello, Carlos 94
Marshall Field 62
McBride, Lloyd 116
McCormick Works 19, 34, 36, 111
Montgomery Ward 62, 111, 115

Oswald, Lee Harvey 94

Panic of 1873 20, 26
Parsons, Albert 27, 33, 34, 36, 39, 41, 44
Pullman, George 50, 51, 59
Pullman (town) 50, 51, 59

Relief and Aid Society 20, 21, 22
Republic Steel 95-108, 116
Reuther, Walter 115
Ruby (Rubinstein), Jack 93, 94, 95

Sadlowski, Ed 116
Sam's Place 97
Sandburg, Carl 83
Shedd. John J. 62
Sinclair, Upton 74
Spies, August 33, 34, 36, 39, 41, 44
Stockyards 70, 72

teachers (Chicago) 124
Tribune 12, 16, 20, 22, 46, 62, 63, 118-122
Turner Hall 20, 30

U.S. Steel 86, 89, 95

WCFL 92
Workingmen's Party of the U.S. 27

Zeigler, Bruce 92